2nd Edition

Living Trust Kit

enodare

by Enodare Publishing

Bibliographic Data

- International Standard Book Number (ISBN): 978-1-906144-66-1
- Printed in the United States of America
- First Printing: April 2011
- Second Edition: January 2014

Published By: Enodare Limited
Athlone
Co. Westmeath
Ireland

Printed & Distributed By: International Publishers Marketing
22841 Quicksilver Drive
Dulles, VA 20166
United States of America

For more information, e-mail books@enodare.com.

Warning and Disclaimer

Although precautions have been taken in the preparation of this kit, neither the publisher nor the author assumes any responsibility for errors or omissions. No warranty of fitness is implied. The information is provided on an "as is" basis. The author and the publisher shall have neither liability nor responsibility to any person or entity with respect to any loss or damages (whether arising by negligence or otherwise) arising from the use of or reliance on the information contained in this kit or from the use of the forms or documents accompanying it.

IMPORTANT NOTE

This kit is meant as a general guide to preparing your own living trust. While considerable effort has been made to make this kit as complete and accurate as possible, laws and their interpretation are constantly changing. As such, you are advised to update this information with your own research and/or advice and to consult with your personal legal, financial and tax advisors before acting on any information contained in this kit.

The purpose of this kit is to educate and entertain. It is not meant to provide legal, financial or tax advice or to create any lawyer-client or advisory relationship. The authors and publisher shall have neither liability (whether in negligence or otherwise) nor responsibility to any person or entity with respect to any loss or damage caused or alleged to be caused directly or indirectly by the information or forms contained in this kit or the use of that information or those forms.

ABOUT ENODARE

Enodare, the international self-help legal publisher, was founded in 2000 by a team including a qualified lawyer. Its aim was simple - to provide access to quality legal information and products at an affordable price.

Enodare's Will Writer software was first published in that year and, following its adaptation to cater for the legal systems of over 30 countries worldwide, quickly drew in excess of 40,000 visitors per month to our website. From this humble start,

Enodare has quickly grown to become a leading international estate planning and asset protection self-help publisher with legal titles in the United States, Canada, Australia, the United Kingdom and Ireland.

Our publications provide customers with the confidence and knowledge to help them deal with everyday estate planning issues such as the preparation of a last will and testament, a power of attorney, a living will, administering an estate and much more.

By providing customers with much needed information and forms, we enable them to protect both themselves and their families through the use of easy to read legal documents and forward planning techniques.

The Future….

We are always seeking to expand and improve the products and services we offer. However, in order to do this, we need to hear from interested authors and to receive feedback from our customers.

If something isn't clear to you in our publications, please let us know and we'll try to make it clearer in the next edition. If you can't find the answer you want and have a suggestion for an addition to our range, we'll happily look at that too.

USING SELF-HELP KITS

Before using a self-help kit, you need to carefully consider the advantages and disadvantages of doing so – particularly where the subject matter is of a legal or tax related nature.

In writing our self-help kits, we try to provide readers with an overview of the laws in a specific area, as well as some sample documents. While this overview is often general in nature, it provides a good starting point for those wishing to carry out a more detailed review of a topic.

However, unlike a lawyer advising a client, we cannot cover every conceivable eventuality that might affect our readers. Within the intended scope of this kit, we can only cover the principal areas in a given topic, and even where we cover these areas, we can still only do so to a moderate extent. To do otherwise would result in the writing of a text book which would be capable of use by legal professionals. This is not what we do.

We try to present useful information and documents that can be used by an average reader with little or no legal knowledge. While our sample documents can be used in the vast majority of cases, everybody's personal circumstances are different. As such, they may not be suitable for everyone. You may have personal circumstances which might impact the effectiveness of these documents or even your desire to use them. The reality is that without engaging a lawyer to review your personal circumstances, this risk will always exist. It's for this very reason that you need to consider whether the cost of using a do-it-yourself legal document outweighs the risk that there may be something special about your particular circumstances which might not be taken into account by the sample documents attached to this kit (or indeed any other sample documents).

It goes without saying (we hope) that if you are in any doubt as to whether the documents in this kit are suitable for use in your particular circumstances, you should contact a suitably qualified lawyer for advice before using them. Remember the decision to use these documents is yours! We are not advising you in any respect.

In using this kit, you should also take into account the fact that this kit has been written with the purpose of providing a general overview of the laws in the United States. As such, it does not attempt to cover all of the various procedural nuances and specific requirements that may apply from state to state – although we do point some of these out along the way. Rather, in our kit, we try to provide forms which give a fair example of the type of forms which are commonly used in most states. Nevertheless, it remains possible that your state may have specific requirements which have not been taken into account in our forms.

Another thing that you should remember is that the law changes – thousands of new laws are brought into force every day and, by the same token, thousands are repealed or amended every day! As such, it is possible that while you are reading this kit, the law might well have been changed. Let's hope it hasn't but the chance does exist! Needless to say, we take regular steps (including e-mail alerts) to update our customers about any changes to the law. We also ensure that our books are reviewed and revised regularly to take account of these changes.

Anyway, assuming that all of the above is acceptable to you, let's move on to exploring the topic at hand.........living trusts

TABLE OF CONTENTS

PROBATE AND WHY PEOPLE TRY TO AVOID IT

Introduction to Probate

Probate is a court supervised administrative process by which the assets of a deceased person (known as a 'decedent') are gathered; applied to pay debts, taxes, and expenses of administration; and then distributed to the beneficiaries named in the decedent's last will and testament.

During the past number of years, a lot has been published about the horrors of probate and the necessity to avoid it. We've all heard desperate stories about the outrageous fees charged by lawyers for carrying out probate – something which is often described as a simple administrative task. You've also probably read articles in the newspaper about the ongoing sufferings of families while they wait for prolonged periods to have their loved one's assets released from probate. In practice however, these are only isolated cases for the most part.

Generally speaking, it's fair to say that more often than not the most immediate concern for dependents when a loved one passes away is the availability of funds to cover the funeral expenses and to discharge ordinary day-to-day living expenses such as mortgages, educational fees, utility bills, grocery bills and so on. Fortunately, given the variety of probate alternatives available, it's quite easy to ensure that not all your assets are tied up in probate following your death and that your loved ones will have immediate access to funds when they need them most. There are a number of these alternatives, the most common of which include life insurance policies, pay-on-death accounts, joint tenancies and trusts.

However, there is little doubt that one of the most popular probate avoidance methods remains the living trust. Indeed, a growing number of elderly people are now turning to living trusts in order to avoid probate – but not only for this reason. Unlike other probate avoidance methods, a living trust has the added advantage of providing a means by which the creator can provide for the management of his or her property during periods of incapacity as well as ensure the privacy of his or her affairs.

However, while there are many compelling reasons to avoid probate, not least of all the avoidance of the excessive cost and long delays usually associated with the process, there are also compelling reasons to engage in the process these reasons include the protection from creditors afforded to the deceased's estate after probate is filed, the ability to appoint guardians under a will and so on. As such, everyone will need to consider what suits their particular circumstances. If you ultimately decide that probate avoidance is for you, then there are a number of probate avoidance measures available to you.

Probate Avoidance Measures

As you may already know, not all of a decedent's assets need to go through probate. Probate can be avoided through the use of a number of legal mechanisms including:-

- payable on death, transfer-on-death or joint accounts;
- insurance policies;
- joint ownership of property;
- lifetime gifts;
- probate free transfers of assets; and
- transfers of motor vehicles.

Of course, if you do not provide for the transfer of all of your assets by means of the above, or indeed any of the other probate avoidance mechanisms, probate will be necessary. We spoke briefly of the advantages and disadvantages of probate in the introduction and, in deciding whether or not you should avoid probate in its entirety, you need to bear these in mind – particularly the advantages of probate.

Pay-on-Death or Transfer-on-Death Accounts

One of easiest ways to avoid probate is by having pay-on-death (POD) and/or transfer-on-death (TOD) accounts. The majority of states now have laws that allow account holders to designate a named beneficiary who will receive the proceeds of their bank and/or investment accounts after they have died. When the account holder dies, the money in the designated account goes directly to the named beneficiary without going through probate. The beneficiary simply needs to bring a death certificate for the account holder to the bank and the bank will arrange the transfer. For more information on these type of accounts, contact your bank.

Transfer-on-Death Securities

The Transfer-on-Death Security Registration Act provides for the transfer-on-death of stocks, shares, bonds and other financial instruments and securities. Similar to the TOD and POD accounts referred to above, these securities can be transferred on death to named beneficiaries free of the requirement to pass through probate. For more information, speak to your broker.

Retirement Accounts

Similar to POD accounts, it's also possible to designate beneficiaries for retirement accounts such as IRAs and 401(k)s. Again, your broker or financial advisor should be able to assist with the designation should you so wish.

Joint Accounts

Another easy way to avoid probate is by having joint accounts. These are similar to pay-on-death accounts. Where an account is held in the name of two or more persons and is designated with the right of survivorship, then when one of the account holders die, the surviving account holder(s) will automatically acquire the deceased account holder's interest in the account. Whoever is the last surviving joint owner will ultimately own the account outright. Where a transfer occurs on survivorship, there is no need for probate. The surviving account holder will simply need to provide a copy of the deceased account holder's death certificate to the bank and the bank can then remove that person's name from the account.

Custodial Accounts

People often decide to set aside funds in the form of bank accounts, certificates of deposit or similar securities as a nest egg for their minor children, grandchildren or others, to cover things like college expenses or simply to give them a start in life. One of the most common ways of doing this is by means of a custodial account. A custodial account is similar to a trust in many ways but is not actually a trust. With a custodial account, the proceeds or assets (where the account is an investment account) are placed under the control of a person known as a custodian. The custodian will have no beneficial interest in the account and will simply manage the account on behalf of the minor beneficiary until they reach a specified age which is determined under state law.

It's important to note that once the custodial account is set up and the beneficiary named, the proceeds of the account then belong to the beneficiary. As a result, the proceeds in custodial accounts will not form part of your probatable estate because the gift is deemed to have been made when the account was set up not when you die or when the custodial account terminates. For further information on custodial accounts, speak to your bank or broker.

Savings Bonds

Saving bonds, like bank accounts, can be held jointly and, like POD accounts, can contain a pay-on-death designation. In the case of jointly held savings bonds, these will pass to the survivor(s) on the death of the other bond holder(s). Similarly, where there is a POD designation, the bonds will pass to the named beneficiary on the death of the bond holder. In each case, probate will not be needed. For further information speak to your bank or financial advisor.

Life Insurance Proceeds

A life policy is another example of a simple means by which you can avoid probate. Where you designate a named beneficiary under your life insurance policy, the proceeds of the policy which are payable on your death will pass directly to the named beneficiary without the need to go through probate. However, if your estate is named as the main beneficiary (which is unusual) or if no beneficiaries have been named or if the named beneficiaries have died, the proceeds will need to pass through probate along with the rest of your probatable estate.

Joint Ownership of Property

Whether or not the property that you own at the time of your death will need to be probated depends on how the title to that property is held. Typically, property can be held in three different ways:-

- joint tenancy (survivorship);

- tenancy by the entireties; and

- tenancy in common.

(i) <u>Joint Tenancy</u>

Where a property is held under a joint tenancy, each of the property owners has an undivided interest in the whole property. They cannot deal with the property in any way without the agreement of the other joint tenants. When one of the joint tenants dies, their share automatically passes to the remaining joint tenants equally without the need to go through probate. All that is then needed is for a lawyer to update the title documents in the local registry of deeds.

(ii) <u>Tenancy By the Entireties</u>

A special type of joint tenancy known as a 'tenancy by the entirety' is recognized between married couples in some states. Under this form of joint ownership, if a married couple owns property as tenants by the entirety, then each spouse has an automatic right of survivorship in that property. This means that when one spouse dies, the other spouse inherits the property automatically without the need to have the property probated. This right can apply to both real estate and the personal assets of the spouses.

Did You Know

States that recognize a 'tenancy by the entirety' include: Alaska*, Arkansas, Delaware, District of Columbia, Florida, Hawaii, Illinois*, Indiana*, Kentucky*, Maryland, Massachusetts, Michigan*, Mississippi, Missouri, New Jersey, New York*, North Carolina*, Ohio, Oklahoma, Oregon, Pennsylvania, Rhode Island, Tennessee, Utah, Vermont, Virginia and Wyoming.

*States that allow tenancy by entirety for real estate only

(iii) <u>Tenancy in Common</u>

A tenancy in common is one of the most common forms of property ownership in most states. A tenancy in common is created where two or more people purchase a property together as 'tenants in common'. As tenants in common, each of the parties own a separate and distinguishable part of the property. As such, each of owners is free to sell their percentage interest in the property to any person at any time and/or to dispose of their interest under their will. The right of survivorship does not apply here.

Lifetime Gifts

Giving away property while alive helps avoid probate since anything that one doesn't own when they die does not go through probate.

Probate Free Transfers of Assets

Any salary, wages, accumulated vacation and sick benefits, plus any other fringe benefits may according to the laws of certain states, be paid to the surviving spouse/partner, adult children or next of kin of the deceased without the need for probate.

Transfer of Vehicles

In nearly all cases ownership of solely owned (by the deceased) vehicles can be transferred immediately to the chosen survivor without requiring probate, including trucks, motor homes and boats. That is, if the total value does not exceed the specified amount of between $25,000 and $75,000 (depending on the state).

The state Department of Motor Vehicles on presentation of a copy of the deceased's death certificate should transfer the title to a vehicle to certain next of kin or alternatively to the person designated by state law. For more information, contact your local Department of Motor Vehicles.

REVOCABLE LIVING TRUSTS

What Are Revocable Living Trusts?

A revocable living trust is a particular type of trust that is used for estate planning purposes. It is a written agreement created for the simple purpose of holding ownership of assets outside of your probatable estate during your lifetime, and then distributing those assets to named beneficiaries after your death.

Specifically, with a living trust, you as the creator of the trust (known as the "grantor") transfer property from your personal ownership to a trust that you have created. You then name yourself as the initial trustee of that trust. The result is that while legal ownership of the trust property changes from you to the trust, you (as initial trustee) continue to maintain control over your property and can continue to enjoy it in same way as you did prior to transferring it to the trust. When you die, a person appointed by you and known as a successor trustee (which is a little like an executor) steps in, takes control of the trust and transfers the trust assets to the people named as beneficiaries under the trust agreement.

Living trusts can be stated to be revocable, meaning that you as the grantor reserve the right to revoke or terminate the trust and resume personal ownership of the trust property at any time. In addition, you maintain discretionary rights, to add to or withdraw assets from the trust property, to change the terms of the trust, and even to make it irrevocable at some time in the future.

Did You Know

Not everyone needs a living trust. As a general rule of thumb, you might conclude that you do not need a living trust where you are young and healthy, you can more easily transfer your assets (or some of them) by other probate avoidance methods or where you do not own any (or very little) property of value. So consider your own situation carefully before making any decision to create a living trust.

Advantages of Living Trusts

There are a number of advantages to using living trusts. These include the following:-

(i)   Avoids Probate

Assets in a living trust are not deemed to be part of your estate and therefore don't need to go through probate when you die. They can be distributed by the successor trustee to your named beneficiaries quickly after your death.

(ii)   Saves Money

By avoiding probate, you will also save your heirs a substantial amount of money in probate fees, filing fees, attorney fees and executor fees.

(iii)   Avoids Publicity

With probate, your will (together with a schedule of all your assets) is filed in the probate registry and becomes a public document open for inspection by anyone upon payment of a small fee. By contrast, a living trust is essentially a private contract entered into between you (as grantor) and yourself (as trustee) and, as there is no public filing requirement, details of your assets and the beneficiaries of same can remain confidential.

(iv)   Provides Protection During Incapacity

With a properly drafted living trust, if you become disabled or otherwise unable to manage your estate, your living trust avoids the need for a court-mandated conservatorship by nominating a person known as a successor trustee (similar to a guardian) to manage the trust assets during any period of incapacity.

(v)   Very Difficult to Contest

As the contents of a living trust are not publicly known, unlike wills, heirs and attorneys are less likely to spend their own time and money pursuing a lawsuit with unknown probabilities of success.

(vi)   Management of Children's Inheritance

It is possible to set up separate sub-trusts within the terms of your living trust for the benefit of young beneficiaries. The terms of these sub-trusts will ordinarily provide that the beneficiary will not inherit the property from the sub-trust until he or she reaches a specified age of your choosing. Until the child or children, as the case may be, reach the designated age, the successor trustee will manage the trust property on their behalf in accordance with the terms of the living trust.

You can also appoint a custodian under the Uniform Transfers to Minors Act to hold and manage assets on behalf of a child beneficiary until that beneficiary reaches an age specified by you in the trust agreement, which will be between 18 and 25 years depending on your state's law.

Did You Know

Remember that, in order to appoint a testamentary guardian to care for your minor children following your death, you will need to make that appointment in your will. You cannot do this in your trust.

(vii)   Flexible

Living trusts are extremely flexible. You can change the terms of the trust, add and withdraw assets, change the beneficiaries of those assets, change the successor trustee or even terminate the trust at any time.

Disadvantages of Living Trusts

There are a number of disadvantages to using living trusts. These include the following:-

(i)   Failure to Fund the Living Trust

One of the biggest problems associated with living trusts is the failure to properly transfer assets into the trust itself. This act of transferring assets is commonly referred to as 'funding the trust'. Where the assets are not properly transferred to the trust, they remain part of your probate estate and are not subject to the terms of your trust. If you have not provided for the transfer of these assets under your will, which is likely, they may end up being unintentionally gifted to the person entitled to the residue of your estate under your will or, where there is no will, to a relative on intestacy.

If any of the assets you propose transferring to your trust have forms of 'title documents' associated with them, you must ensure that the title is properly transferred from your personal name into the name of the trust.

(ii)   <u>Doesn't Completely Avoid Delays in the Distribution of Assets</u>

One of the main reasons for delays in the probate process is caused by the necessity to resolve complicated tax issues before distributing assets to the beneficiaries of the deceased person's estate. The same problem exists in relation to a living trust as a person is taxed as if the living trust doesn't exist. In other words, for tax purposes you will be deemed to own the assets in the living trust personally, while for probate purposes you will not. Your successor trustee could therefore have to wait until probate is complete (or at least that part relating to the payment of taxes) before distributing the gifts under the living trust.

Another common problem stems from the collection of assets, in particular life insurance proceeds. It can take months to obtain these proceeds, and again the problem exists both for an executor appointed under a will and a successor trustee appointed under a living trust.

(iii)   <u>Lack of Court Supervision</u>

One of the benefits of the probate system is that the court often watches over the distribution of your estate and, in doing so, protects the interests of your beneficiaries. However, no such supervision occurs with a living trust as the responsibility for effecting and overseeing the distribution of your trust assets rests solely with your designated successor trustee. This can be disadvantageous in certain circumstances.

(iv)   <u>Limited Financial Savings for Smaller Estates</u>

The real determination as to whether a living trust will save you money depends on how much probate fees would have been paid had the trust assets gone through probate rather than passing through your living trust. If the estate has a small monitory value, you may find that the probate fees payable in your state are quite low having regard to the costs of establishing and maintaining a living trust.

(v)   <u>No Protection from Creditors</u>

One of the principal drawbacks from not going through the probate process is that no time limit is imposed on creditors within which they can take claims against your estate. With probate, all creditors must notify the executor of any claim they have within a specified time limit. If they fail to notify the executor on time, their claim becomes statute barred and they cannot recover against the estate or your trust. The opposite is the case with living trusts. No time limit is imposed on your creditors and, as such, they can take claims against you or your estate well after you have died. Moreover, even when the trust is wound up and the assets distributed to the beneficiaries of the trust, they have the right in many states to sue the beneficiaries for the debts you owed – up to the maximum of the benefit they received.

For the above reason, it's often quite useful to have some asset go through the probate process in order to restrict the rights of creditors to take action against your estate and your trust.

Types of Living Trust

The two main types of living trusts used for estate planning purposes are basic living trusts and AB Trusts. A basic living trust, which can be used by an individual or a couple, has the primary objective of avoiding probate. An AB Trust, on the other hand, goes one step further by saving on estate taxes. We'll discuss the basic types of trust only below as the AB trust generally only applies to people with assets worth in excess of $10,680,000 – people who will have substantive estate planning needs.

Living Trust for an Individual

If you're single, you probably want your living trust to transfer your property to your relatives and friends following your death. If this is the case, then the basic living trust could be right for you. As already explained, to create a basic living trust you simply sign a trust agreement between yourself as grantor and yourself as trustee. Under the terms of the trust agreement you will nominate someone to act as your successor trustee and also specify who is to receive the benefit of your trust assets following your death. When you die, your successor trustee steps in and transfers the trust property to the beneficiaries named in your living trust.

If you have any children, you can use your trust to leave property to them; with care of that property being vested in a property guardian or trustee until they reach the age you have specified in your trust agreement.

Living Trusts for Couples

Couples, whether married or not, often own property together. If you are part of a couple, you can decide whether you want to create an individual trust for your own separate property or whether you want to create a joint or shared living trust with your partner.

If you are married or in a registered domestic partnership, then you will need to consider and take into account whether you are living in a community property state or whether you are living in a common law state. In brief, depending on what state you are living in, the law will determine what amounts to your individual property and what amounts to joint marital property. You can transfer your individual property to a living trust as well as your share of your community property.

Unless you and your spouse or registered domestic partner individually have assets worth more than $5,340,000 (or with a combined worth in excess of $10,680,000 - in which case some tax planning would be required) there are two principal types of living trust arrangement that couples can create:

- Each spouse or partner prepares their own individual living trust; or

- Both of you prepare one shared living trust.

We discuss each arrangement in detail below.

- *Individual Living Trusts*

    For couples, the use of individual trusts can make a lot of sense where you and your spouse/partner own most of your property separately rather than jointly. In such cases, you may want to ensure that your spouse or partner does not gain control over your assets once you transfer them to the trust while at the same time ensuring that your assets are not tied up in probate. An individual trust is ideal in such circumstances.

However, there are drawbacks to using individual living trusts. For example, in order to transfer a jointly held asset into a trust, it may become necessary to divide title to the asset into two separate deeds and thereafter have each spouse transfer their half of the asset to their trust. This can become expensive and messy and sometimes, in such circumstances, it makes sense to create an additional trust to hold the jointly held assets. For this reason, it is often recommended that couples avoid individual trusts in favor of shared living trusts. Of course the choice is yours!

- *Basic Shared Living Trusts*

Many couples use one basic shared living trust to avoid probate and to handle both their co-owned property and their separately held property. Here, both partners establish the trust and as such, both act as co-grantors and co-trustees of the trust. As co-grantors, each partner can nominate beneficiaries for their individual or separate property and for their portion of joint property. In addition, each partner can unilaterally call for the return of their assets to them and/or revoke the trust at any time. When the trust is revoked, the assets return to the parties that placed them in the trust. Each partner retains full ownership and control of all their separate property as well as their share of the jointly owned property.

When one of the partners dies, the trust automatically splits into two separate trusts – we'll call them the 'first trust' and the 'second trust'. The deceased partner's property and share of the joint property is automatically transferred in to the first trust. The terms of the first trust immediately become irrevocable which means the surviving partner cannot amend them in any way. Thereafter, the surviving partner in his/her capacity as successor trustee distributes the property in the first trust in accordance with the deceased partner's wishes as set out in the trust document. In many cases, the deceased partner will leave his or her assets to the surviving partner's trust – the second trust.

All of the remaining trust assets are transferred to the second trust, which continues to exist as a stand-alone trust – similar to an individual trust. This trust is revocable by the surviving partner in the same way as an individual trust. When the surviving partner dies, the trust assets will be distributed in accordance with the terms of the trust in the usual way.

Conclusion

You should carefully consider the use of each of the above types of trust before deciding that any of them would suit your particular circumstances. Remember, as well as the advantages, each comes with its own set of particular disadvantages. You should choose wisely and tailor any living trust to your own, unique circumstances.

TRUSTEES AND SUCCESSOR TRUSTEES

The Initial Trustee

When it comes to living trusts, you will usually appoint yourself as the initial trustee of the trust. Where there are two grantors, such as in the case of a shared or joint trust, both grantors are usually appointed as co-trustees. Allowing grantors to serve as the initial trustees is a key feature of revocable living trusts as the whole purpose behind a living trust is to bypass probate in a manner which allows the grantors the right to retain complete freedom to deal with and control the assets which are transferred to the trust.

Appointing a Co-Trustee

You may decide, for whatever reason, that rather than hand over the management of your trust assets to another person entirely, you would simply like to engage someone to assist in the management of your trust property. You can do this quite easily by appointing someone as a co-trustee of your trust. As co-trustees, both of you would have authority to act on the trust's behalf. While there is no real difficulty with having someone else act as trustee of your trust or even have someone act as a co-trustee, we recommend that you speak to a lawyer before you do this as the terms of your trust document may need to be tailored to cater for this eventuality.

Successor Trustees

Your successor trustee is the person who assumes control of the trust after you, as initial trustee, become incapacitated and/or die. In the case of a shared or joint trust, your successor trustee will take over control of the trust when both trustees are incapacitated or dead. A successor trustee has no authority to act while any of the grantors remain alive or capable of managing the trust. Your trust deed will identify the person or persons who will act as successor trustee(s) of your trust. In most cases, this is usually a relative or a family friend.

It is important to note that even though you name someone in the trust agreement to act as successor trustee, he or she is under absolutely no obligation to carry out the role and cannot be forced to do so. It is open to anyone named as the successor trustee to decline to act. Where this happens, the next named successor trustee will take over the management and administration of the trust. If no alternate is named or none of the named alternates are willing to serve, the beneficiaries of the trust will need to petition the local court to appoint someone to fill the role unless they have authority under the trust agreement to appoint a replacement successor trustee.

One of the most important aspects of your living trust is your choice of successor trustee(s). Do not choose a trustee just because they are a family member or close friend — choose someone that you trust implicitly; someone that you know is competent and capable of handling the demands of a successor trustee's role. You also need to choose someone who is honestly willing to do the job for you.

Changing Trustees

While you are alive, you can amend the trust deed to change the proposed trustee at any time. However, in order to deal with the changing of trustees after your death, specific provisions will need to be inserted into your trust deed. For example, where a successor trustee wishes to resign you should include provisions to ensure an orderly transition from the resigning trustee to a successor trustee. In this regard, you could require that the resignation of a trustee will not become effective until at least fourteen to thirty days after written notice of the resignation has been given to you, if living, or to the current trust beneficiaries of the trust, if you are not living. These notice requirements will ensure that you or the trust beneficiaries of the trust have sufficient time to have a successor trustee in place before the resigning trustee actually resigns.

GIFTS AND BENEFICIARIES

Types of Gifts under a Living Trust

A gift is a voluntary transfer of property by one person to another made gratuitously, without any consideration or compensation. In your living trust, you may leave gifts of financial or personal value to your family and friends after you pass away. Gifts can come in the form of specific item gifts, cash gifts or a gift of the residuary of your trust estate.

Specific Item Gifts

These gifts include specific items of property which you have transferred into your trust such as, for example, a car, a piece of jewelry, stocks, bonds and real estate. Needless to say, when drafting your living trust, it's important that you clearly identify and describe the property that you wish to gift. So, for example, where you are gifting a car, you should describe the make, model and color of the car rather than simply referring to "my car". This reduces the risk of confusion over what you intended – especially if you have transferred more than one car into your living trust. When writing a provision for a gift, a good question to ask yourself is whether a stranger reviewing the terms of your living trust would easily understand exactly what you wanted to gift. If not, you need to re-write that clause.

Cash Gifts

A cash gift is a gift of a specific amount of money or cash to a named beneficiary. Just as with specific items gifts, when making a cash gift you need to clearly specify the amount that you are gifting (including the currency), and the person to whom you wish to gift.

Gift of the Residuary Trust Estate

The residue of your trust estate (or residuary trust estate, as it is often called) is the remainder of the trust assets in the trust after the payment of all debts, expenses, specific gifts and cash gifts have been made. A residuary estate also includes property that is the subject of a failed gift. A gift fails in circumstances where the beneficiary has died (and no alternate beneficiary is named to receive the gift) or refuses to accept the gift. The person entitled to receive a gift of the residuary trust estate under your living trust is called the residuary beneficiary or, if there is more than one beneficiary, residuary beneficiaries.

What Is a Beneficiary?

A beneficiary is a person, organization or other entity who will inherit part of your trust assets under the terms of your living trust.

Generally speaking, you are more or less free to decide who you gift your trust assets to. Typically, people tend to leave avssets to their spouse, children, siblings, relatives, friends, charities and even their local church. However, while you are largely free to gift your assets as you wish, you also need to be careful of those to whom you might not leave any assets. For example, if you decide to disinherit a spouse, they may be able to successfully sue your estate and/or your living trust after your death and obtain an order providing for a redistribution of your assets to include an appropriate share for them. We'll discuss this point further below.

It is also worthwhile noting that in most states restrictions are imposed on minor beneficiaries owning assets. Specifically, a child will be prohibited from owning significant assets until he or she has reached the age of majority in their state. Where a child is named as a beneficiary under the terms of a living trust the assets gifted to the child are usually placed in to the care of a trustee or guardian who will hold them in trust until such time as the child is old enough to take control of the assets in his or her own right.

Types of Beneficiaries under a Living Trust

There are three principal types of beneficiaries under a living trust. These include a specific gift beneficiary, an alternate beneficiary, and a residuary beneficiary.

Specific Gift Beneficiary

A specific gift beneficiary is a person or organization named in your living trust to receive a specific item of property from your trust estate. These items of property tend to include items such as sums of money, jewelry, stocks etc.

Alternate Beneficiary

When naming a person to receive a gift or the residue of your trust estate under your living trust, it's prudent to prepare for the possibility that one or more of your beneficiaries will be unable or unwilling (for whatever reason) to accept the gift/residue. It is therefore helpful to nominate an alternate beneficiary. An alternate beneficiary is a person who becomes legally entitled to inherit the gift/residue if the first named beneficiary is unable or unwilling to accept the gift/residue.

Residuary Beneficiary

A residuary beneficiary is the person(s) or organization(s) named to receive the residue of the trust estate. As mentioned above, the residue of the trust estate is that part of the trust estate which remains after the payment of all debts and expenses, and after the transfer of all specific gifts.

Beneficiaries under a Shared Trust

Remember, with a basic shared living trust, each partner/spouse has the ability to name his or her own beneficiaries quite separately from their partner/spouse. When one of the partners dies, the surviving partner will distribute the deceased partner's separate property and their share of the joint property in accordance with the terms of the living trust. The property of the surviving spouse will remain under a separate revocable living trust for the benefit of the surviving spouses.

Gifts to Spouses

Before making a gift to your spouse, it is important to understand the basic differences in distribution of property in both common law property states and community property states. These differences will determine what portion of your overall estate (if any) you are obliged to transfer to your spouse.

Community Property States

Property owned by couples in community property states is divided loosely into two categories: separate property and community property.

Separate property is all property acquired by a spouse/partner before or after a marriage (including after a legal separation) or entry into a civil partnership plus all property received as a gift or an inheritance and maintained separately (i.e. not jointly with their spouse) during the marriage/partnership. Community property, on the other hand, is all other property earned or acquired by either spouse or registered domestic partner during a marriage/partnership.

Did You Know

At the date of writing there are nine community property states namely Arizona, California, Idaho, Louisiana, Nevada, New Mexico, Texas, Washington, and Wisconsin. In Alaska couples can opt to have their property treated as community property under the terms of a written property agreement.

Separate property can also be deemed community property where it is formerly transferred to the joint names of both spouses. Similarly, where seperate property is gifted to one spouse and commingled with community property, the property can become community property.

Alaska, Arizona, California, Nevada, Texas and Wisconsin each allow a surviving spouse or domestic partner to automatically inherit community property when the other spouse or partner dies provided that property's title document makes it clear that the property is owned as community property with a right of survivorship in favor of the surviving spouse/partner.

Normally, classifying property as community or separate property is relatively straightforward. However there are a number of instances in which the classification is not clear. These include valuations of businesses, companies, pensions, the proceeds of certain lawsuits, and incomes received from separate property. In each case, you should consult a local attorney to determine how your state treats these items.

The majority of community property states do not grant a surviving spouse a legal right to inherit from the deceased spouse's estate. Rather, what they do is try to divide the marital assets (or registered partnership assets) during the lifetime of the spouses by classifying certain assets as community property. Each spouse in turn has a right to 50% of the community property. This needs to be remembered when designating beneficiaries for assets.

However, in each of Alaska, California, Idaho, Washington and Wisconsin a surviving spouse or domestic partner may elect to receive a specific portion of the deceased spouse's community or separate property in limited circumstances. For more information on such entitlements, we recommend that you consult a lawyer.

Important Note

If you are in a registered domestic partnership and considering a move to another state, you should pay close attention to laws of the state into which you are proposing to move as the 'new state' may not recognize the property rights which you had in your 'old state'. If you are in any doubt as to how the law will affect you, you should consult a practicing lawyer in your area.

Common Law States

In common law states, each spouse owns all property acquired using their own income and all property legally registered solely in their name. In a common law state, any property, such as your marital home for example, that is registered in the names of you and your spouse is deemed to be owned jointly. If you reside in a common law state, your spouse has a legal right to a fraction of your estate upon your passing. Depending on the state in question, this legal right will usually amount to between one-third and one-half of your estate. The precise amount to which your spouse is entitled will also depend on whether you have any minor children and whether your spouse has been provided for outside the terms of your living trust (e.g. under your will).

The legal right of your spouse will take priority over any devises or legacies made in your will or your living trust, and ranks in priority after creditors of your estate. Your spouse is entitled to exercise his/her legal right to receive the specified fraction of your estate which they are entitled to under law or they can waive this right in favor of whatever has been left to them under the terms of your will or your living trust. The right of your spouse to take a percentage of your estate does not arise by operation of the law; rather it must be proactively elected. Your surviving spouse can, therefore, waive any entitlement to receive their legal right share.

In certain states, your surviving spouse may have an additional right to inherit the family home or, in certain cases, a right to live there for a defined period (which may be life). In some states, your spouse might even be entitled to day-to-day living expenses during the probate of your estate.

Matters can become more complex when a couple moves from a common law state to a community property state. In California, Idaho, Washington and Wisconsin, property acquired prior to a move will be treated as if it had been acquired in the state to which you have moved. In other community property states, the property will be treated in accordance with the laws of the state in which it was acquired. As you no doubt have gathered, this can result in marital property being subjected to both common law and community property rules. In such cases, it is important that care is taken to determine which laws affect what types of property before you commence transferring property to your living trust or otherwise.

By contrast, couples that move from a community property state to a common law state come up against the opposite problem. In such cases, each spouse retains a 50% interest in the community property acquired while the couple was resident in the community property state.

CHILDREN, GUARDIANS AND PROPERTY MANAGEMENT

Management of Children's Property

Depending on your state's laws, minor children may only receive a nominal amount of property in to their own names under the terms of a will or living trust. The amount varies between approximately $1,000 and $5,000 depending on the state in question. If you leave a gift to a minor in excess of the permitted statutory amount, it will be necessary either by the terms of your trust or by a court order to appoint an adult called a "custodian", "trustee" or "property guardian" to receive and manage the property on behalf of the child.

Fortunately, it is relatively easy and straightforward to appoint someone to manage any property that a minor or young adult will inherit from you. While there are many ways that you can structure this arrangement, two of the simplest and most commonly used methods are listed below.

Uniform Transfer to Minors' Act

As often mentioned, minors in most states do not have the legal capacity to enter into certain legal contracts, and are therefore not in a position where they can own and manage assets such as stocks, bonds, funds, life insurance receipts and other annuities. It is therefore important to recognize that you cannot simply transfer any of these types of items directly to your minor children; or indeed to any other minor.

One of the most common methods used to get around this problem comes in the form of a custodianship created under the Uniform Transfer to Minors Act ("UTMA"). Rather than transferring assets directly to a young beneficiary on your death, you transfer your assets to a custodian who will hold those assets on trust for the beneficiary until they reach a pre-determined age. Once the beneficiary reaches this age, the custodian will transfer the property that he or she is holding on their behalf to them. In the interim period, the custodian will be obliged to manage the property on the beneficiary's behalf in accordance with the provisions set out in the UTMA.

To set up a custodianship, all you need to do is identify the property which you want to transfer to a young beneficiary and to name a custodian to manage that property in the event that the beneficiary in question had not reached a designated age (usually between 18 to 25 years depending on state law) at the time they became entitled to receive the gift.

A typical clause of this type would be as follows:-

> *"I give $25,000 to James Jones, as custodian for Sarah Parker under the California Uniform Transfers to Minors Act, to hold until Sarah Parker reaches the age of 21 years."*

The UTMA has been adopted in all states except for Vermont and South Carolina.

The age at which the custodianship terminates is the age at which a minor becomes legally entitled to call for the assets held by a custodian to be transferred to him or her, and to have the custodial trust terminated. The table below shows the ages of termination of custodianships in the various states which have adopted the UTMA. As you will see, the ages vary from 18 to 25 years of age. You will also see that in some states the age is specified, while in other states a range of ages is provided from which the grantor can chose a particular age. You should be aware that the age of termination of a custodianship is not necessarily the same as the age of majority in a particular state.

State	UGMA	UTMA	UGMA Repeal *
Alabama	19	21	October 1, 1986
Alaska	18	18-25	January 1, 1991
Arizona	18	21	September 30, 1988
Arkansas	21	18-21	March 21, 1985
California	18	18-25	January 1, 1985
Colorado	21	21	July 1, 1984
Connecticut	21	21	October 1, 1995
Delaware	18	21	June 26, 1996
District of Columbia	18	18-21	March 12, 1986
Florida	18	21	October 1, 1985
Georgia	21	21	July 1, 1990

State	UGMA	UTMA	UGMA Repeal *
Guam	21	N/A	N/A
Hawaii	18	21	July 1, 1985
Idaho	18	21	July 1, 1984
Illinois	21	21	July 1, 1986
Indiana	18	21	July 1, 1989
Iowa	21	21	July 1, 1986
Kansas	18	21	July 1, 1985
Kentucky	21	18	July 15, 1986
Louisiana	18	18	January 1, 1988
Maine	21	18-21	August 4, 1988
Maryland	18	21	July 1, 1989
Massachusetts	18	21	January 30, 1987
Michigan	18	18-21	December 29, 1999
Minnesota	18	21	January 1, 1986
Mississippi	21	21	January 1, 1995
Missouri	21	21	September 28, 1985
Montana	18	21	October 1, 1985
Nebraska	19	21	July 15, 1992
Nevada	18	18-25	July 1, 1985
New Hampshire	21	21	July 30, 1985
New Jersey	21	18-21	July 1, 1987
New Mexico	21	21	July 1, 1989
New York	18	21	July 10, 1996
North Carolina	18	18-21	October 1, 1987
North Dakota	18	21	July 1, 1985
Ohio	18	18-21	May 7, 1986
Oklahoma	21	18-21	November 1, 1986
Oregon	21	21-25	January 1, 1986
Pennsylvania	21	21-25	December 16, 1992
Rhode Island	21	21	July 23, 1998
South Carolina	18	N/A	N/A
South Dakota	18	18	July 1, 1986

State	UGMA	UTMA	UGMA Repeal *
Tennessee	18	21-25	October 1, 1992
Texas	18	21	September 1, 1995
Utah	21	21	July 1, 1990
Vermont	18	N/A	N/A
Virgin Islands	21	N/A	N/A
Virginia	18	18-21	July 1, 1988
Washington	21	21	July 1, 1991
West Virginia	18	21	July 1, 1986
Wisconsin	18	21	April 8, 1988
Wyoming	18	21	May 22, 1987

Child Sub-Trusts

A 'child's sub-trust' is valid in all U.S. states and can be created under the terms of a living trust. In your living trust agreement, you simply make a gift to the beneficiary and then nominate the successor trustee to manage the inheritance that the beneficiary will receive until that beneficiary reaches an age specified by you. If the beneficiary in question has reached that age at the time of your death, and is past the age of majority for his or her state, the trust never actually comes into existence and the property is instead transferred directly to the beneficiary upon your death.

However, where the beneficiary is under the age specified in your trust agreement, the inheritance will be transferred to a separate trust fund and will be managed by the successor trustee in accordance with the provisions set out in the trust agreement. The successor trustee will continue to manage the trust property until the beneficiary in question has reached the age specified in your trust document. At that time, the remainder of the trust property will be transferred to the beneficiary and the trust will be terminated.

While this type of trust is commonly called a 'child's sub-trust' you are in fact free to specify the age at which the beneficiary shall become entitled to receive his or her inheritance from the trustee. You could therefore create a trust for someone that is already 35 years old and provide that they will not receive their inheritance until they are 40 years old. In reality, however, most people provide that the beneficiary should be entitled to receive their inheritances between the ages of 18 and 40 years. Obviously, if there are concerns over whether the beneficiary is mature enough to manage his or her inheritance, the age at which he or she shall become entitled to receive the trust assets can remain high.

During the course of the trust, the trustee will have broad discretion over the management and distribution of the trust property. If the trustee deems it appropriate, he or she can release monies to or make payments on behalf of the beneficiary to cover matters ranging from education, medical and general maintenance.

While court supervision is generally not required with these types of trusts, serving as a trustee can be more onerous than simply serving as a custodian under the UTMA. For example, a trustee is required to file annual income tax returns for each child trust with the IRS. Also, because the powers of the trustee of a child's sub-trust are set out in the trust agreement itself, it may be necessary for the trustee to produce copies of the relevant document every time he or she has to deal with a financial institution. By contrast, given that the powers of a UTMA custodian are provided for under statute, the majority of banks and other institutions are more familiar with their terms and are more knowledgeable of the authority given to custodians under these statutes -thereby making dealings a lot easier.

TRANSFERRING ASSETS TO YOUR LIVING TRUST

Transfer of Assets

As already mentioned, there are two primary reasons why you might establish a revocable living trust. Firstly you want to provide for the management of your property during any period of incapacity. Secondly, you may want to avoid the costs and delays associated with having your assets go through the probate process. Both are perfectly legitimate and solid reasons for establishing your living trust. However, if having established the trust you fail to properly transfer assets to the trust, or fund the trust as the term is called, your efforts will have been in vain. Without complying with the required formalities to transfer assets to your trust, these assets will be deemed to be your personal assets and will end up going through the probate process; or the intestate administration process if you have failed to make a last will and testament - which deals with these assets.

What Assets should be put in Your Living Trust?

One of the principal goals of any living trust is to avoid the cost associated with probate, with the general rule being that the more an asset is worth, the more it will cost your estate on probate fees. It follows therefore that you should, at the very least, consider transferring your most valuable assets to you living trust. However, it is entirely up to you what you decide to include or leave out.

You are free to include assets such as your home and other real estate, bank and saving accounts, investments, business interests, antiques, jewelry, personal belongings, royalties, patents, copyrights, stocks, bonds and other securities, money market accounts and so on.

In deciding what assets you want to transfer to your living trust, always bear in mind that where you are acting as both the grantor and trustee of your own trust, you always have the right to call for the return of any or all of the assets you transfer into the trust.

The reality is that you don't need to put everything into your living trust in order to save money on probate. For example, you don't need to include assets which do not go through the probate process.

Title to Assets Transferred to a Living Trust

While there has been considerable debate as to whether property transferred to a living trust needs to be re-titled in the name of the trust, we recommend that all assets which have any form of title document should be re-titled in the name of the trust. To transfer assets which do not have title documents to your trust, all you typically need to do is simply list them in the schedule of assets contained at the back of your trust agreement.

In order to re-register the title of an asset from your personal name in to the name of your living trust, you simply sign a document transferring the legal title in that asset from you to the trust. The transfer will be between, for example, John Smith and John Smith, trustee of the John Smith Family living trust dated 1 January 2014. Then when it comes to signing the transfer document, you will sign the document in your own right as (for example) "John Smith" AND you will also sign on behalf of the living trust using the words "John Smith, Trustee" or something similar.

Any failure to properly transfer the asset can result in it remaining as part of your probate estate.

Transferring Property to Your Trust

Given the vast diversity of assets that you can transfer to your living trust, we will take a very brief look below at some of the most commonly transferred assets and how those transfers should be effected so as to ensure that they become part of your trust estate.

Real Estate

In order to transfer real estate into your living trust you will need to prepare a deed of transfer. In most cases this can be pretty straightforward. However, there are certain issues that you need to watch out for as there are many different nuances associated with the transfer of title to real estate – such as the type of deed required, title insurance, mortgages, out-of-state property, homestead rights and tax on transfer deeds. As such, we recommend that you engage the services of an attorney qualified in your state to assist with the transfer of any property located in your state.

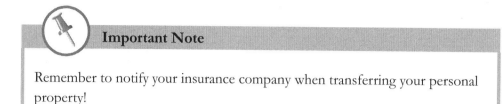

Important Note

Remember to notify your insurance company when transferring your personal property!

Cars, Boats and Other Vehicles

You can transfer a vehicle to your trust in much the same way as you would transfer it to a third party. However, many of these assets can also be passed without the need to go through probate so check with the local registrar of vehicles before you make a decision on what to transfer to and what to leave out of your living trust.

You should note that the majority of states have a specific form that can be used for registering the transfer of a vehicle.

Cash Accounts

In order to transfer the title to your current (checking) accounts, savings accounts or money market accounts you can either change the name on the account (from "John Smith" to "John Smith, trustee of John Smith Family living trust", for example) or close the account and open a new one in the name of the trust. Each financial institution can advise on which of the two methods they will allow.

United States Savings Bonds

While U.S. Savings bonds can be transferred into your living trust, you will need to contact your bank to obtain the appropriate form to transfer the bonds as well as details of the procedure involved. Once the transfer is completed, the bonds will be re-issued in the name of your living trust.

Broker Accounts

It is also possible to transfer a broker account held with a brokerage firm or with a mutual fund company to your living trust. Similar to the position with bank accounts, you will need to contact the firm/company to determine whether they can simply change the name on the account or whether they will have to close the existing account and open a new one in the name of the trust.

Publicly Quoted Stocks and Bonds

There are two ways to transfer stock in a publicly quoted company to your living trust. You can contact the company's share registrar (or transfer agent as it's often called) or you can contact your broker and ask him to open an account in the name of the living trust and have the stock re-issued to the trust.

Retirement Plans

Due to their complexity, tax advantages and unique distribution features pension plans, profit-sharing plans, IRSs, Keoghs, SEPs and other qualified pension plans should never be transferred into a living trust without first consulting your tax advisor.

Other Property

If you want to transfer any other property to your living trust, a simple deed of assignment should suffice. However, if there are specific documents required to effect transfers of property (such as share or stock transfer forms for a corporation) then you should use the required form. If you are uncertain as to how to proceed, we suggest that you contact an attorney.

Finally remember, you can transfer assets out of your living trust and back to you by simply reversing the process outlined above. As grantor and trustee, you ordinarily have full authority and capacity to do this.

MAKING, AMENDING & REVOKING YOUR LIVING TRUST

Making Your Living Trust

Now that you've had time to think about who you will appoint as your successor trustee, what assets you can and want to transfer to your trust and who will ultimately receive those assets, it's time to start putting the plan in to progress.

As you will see, we have included a number of sample living trust forms at the back of this book. However, before using our forms, there are several very important steps which you must follow. The good news is that none of these steps are overly difficult. However, they must be followed. Otherwise you run the risk on not property creating or funding your living trust – and we've already touched on the impact that could have.

The steps are set out below. Feel free to refer to them as often as you wish.

1.   Read through this book very carefully. By doing this you will gain an overview of the entire process and will have a much better understanding as to how your living trust will operate and whether or not a living trust is actually for you.

2.   Fill in the Living Trust Worksheet contained at Appendix 1. This is designed to help compile the information required for insertion into your living trust. Information regarding your assets, beneficiaries, preferred trustees and many other items will be gathered together in this worksheet for your use. While you may not notice it, as you fill in this worksheet, you will start to make the actual decisions regarding the assets you want to include in your living trust and how you want to distribute them. The worksheet will also help you select both a successor trustee and an alternate successor trustee.

3.   Next, you will need to review your own state's legal requirements relating to living trusts. You can do this on the internet or by reviewing the State Law Digest which sets out a concise listing of the laws relating to living trusts in every state. While the standard clauses in our living trust agreements cover most of the potential issues that may arise, there may well be other nuances

of state law which could impact your decision to use a living trust – just check to be sure!

4.   Select the form from Appendix 3 which appears most suitable to your circumstances. Read through the form carefully. While the form is relatively straight forward, you should never sign a legal document without first reading it in its entirety and fully understanding it. If you are in any doubt as to what something means contact an attorney.

You should carefully follow the procedure and instructions set out in Appendix 2 in order to fill in the appropriate information on your chosen living trust form. You should use the information set out in your Living Trust Worksheet to assist you in this task.

6.   Once completed, proof read your entire living trust agreement to ensure that there are no omissions or typographical errors, and that all provisions are written exactly as you require - especially the gift section.

7.   In order to execute your completed living trust, follow the procedures set out in Appendix 2.

8.   You should give a photocopy of your original, signed living trust to your successor trustee as he or she may need to act during any period in which you are incapacitated. Keep the original in a safe place.

That's all there is to it.

Resource

For more information on obtaining wallet cards and storing your advance directives electronically so that physicians and medical personnel can easily access them in a time of emergency we recommend visiting the Legal Vaults™ website at www.legalvaults.com.

Reviewing Your Living Trust

In the same way as you would ordinarily review your finances or health regularly, it's important that you review important legal documents such as your living trust and your last will and testament regularly. We recommend that you carry out this review every year or, at the least every two to three years. In addition, we recommend that you carry out a similar review whenever there is a major change to your personal or financial position – such as in the case of a birth, death or divorce in your family or in the case of a substantial appreciation or depreciation in your financial position.

Depending on the change in question, it may be necessary to actually amend the terms of your living trust. We'll discuss this in detail under the next heading.

Amending Your Living Trust

Important Note

One of the advantages of a revocable living trust is that you can amend or revoke it at any time!

As suggested above, there may well be events which require you to amend the terms of your living trust. The most common reasons why you might want to amend your living trust include:-

- a change in your marital status;
- a move to another state;
- you adopt or have a new child;
- your child becomes an adult;
- a material change to your financial position or the value of your trust assets;
- a major change in tax law;
- one of your beneficiaries passes away;
- you wish to add a new beneficiary or change existing beneficiaries; or
- one of your successor trustees dies or is unable or unwilling to serve.

If any of the above events occur, or indeed any other event which is unlisted, you may wish to change the terms of your trust. The process of amending your living trust is quite easy. All you need to do is complete an amendment agreement. Similar to the living trust agreement, the amendment agreement will be between you as grantor and you as trustee of your living trust. An amendment agreement typically provides for the deletion of one clause or sentence in your living trust and the inclusion of another clause or clauses instead.

For a Living Trust Amendment Kit, simply visit the Enodare.com website.

Transferring or Removing Property from Your Living Trust

We have already covered the transfer of property to your living trust. However, it is also worth mentioning here that if you want to add any additional property to your living trust, all you need to do is to sign the required transfer document and update the schedule contained at the back of your living trust agreement. Alternatively, if you want to remove property held by the trust and place it back in your personal possession, you again execute a transfer document and update the schedule – this time operating in reverse so that the trust is the transferor and you, personally, are the transferee. It's that easy!

Revocation of Your Living Trust

While it's not too common an occurrence, a living trust can be revoked at any time. In order to revoke a living trust, you must do the following:-

- Firstly, you must, in your capacity as grantor, prepare and serve a notice of revocation on the trustee of the trust (which is generally the grantor). The notice will inform that trustee that the trust is terminated and will call for the return of the trust assets to the grantor. We have included a sample notice of revocation at Appendix 6.

- Secondly, you must arrange for the transfer of legal title in the trust assets to be transferred from the living trust back to the grantor personally. We have discussed this process above.

- Thirdly, ensure that any beneficiary designations in favor of the living trust should be amended. In this respect, we are talking about pay-on-death accounts, life insurance, etc.

- It's important to note that with a shared living trust, notwithstanding that there are normally two co-grantors, either co-grantor alone is legally entitled to terminate the trust by service of a notice of revocation.

OTHER ANCILLARY DOCUMENTS REQUIRED

Pour-Over Wills

A pour-over will is a special type of will that is used in conjunction with a living trust. Instead of providing for the distribution of all of your assets and property, the pour-over will simply provides that any of your property that has not been transferred into your living trust before your death will 'pour-over' into your living trust after you die. In this way, it ensures that these assets will be distributed in accordance with the provisions set out in your living trust.

In essence a pour-over will is like most other wills. It provides for the revocation of other wills, names an executor and appoints a guardian for minor children. The one real difference is that it has one specific beneficiary – your living trust.

While a pour-over will has certain advantages, the major drawback is that the property passing under the will may have to go through probate. This in turn means that the beneficiaries of your living trust have to wait for probate to complete before the assets are transferred to the trust. They will also have to wait for the successor trustee to make the distribution from the living trust. The chances of a speedy distribution in those circumstances are slim unless the grantor's probatable estate outside the living trust is small enough to avail of the expedited procedures available for the probate of 'small estates'.

Notwithstanding the above, the use of a pour-over will can be beneficial where circumstances exist which deter people from putting all of their property into their living trusts during their lifetimes. For example, due to restrictions imposed by certain states and insurance companies, it can often be difficult to buy, sell, or insure assets held in a living trust.

In other situations, people who have established living trusts simply forget to transfer all of their assets to the trust or don't get an opportunity to do so. For example, someone might have received an inheritance a few days before they pass away and simply never had an opportunity during their last days to make the transfer.

The use of a pour-over will is therefore a good means by which to avoid intestacy and have state law determine how your assets should be divided. Similarly, there is no reason why you cannot simply have a will of your own with a standard residuary clause which mirrors that set out in the living trust – it more or less accomplishes the same thing in most instances. However, there may be situations where, under the terms of a living trust, the residuary trust estate is passed to a minor beneficiary and a sub-trust is set up in the living trust to cater for the management of the child's property until he or she is sufficiently old to take control of the property. In such circumstances, it makes sense to flow the excess assets into the living trust rather than providing for a separate trust for the same child under the terms of your will

All in all, it is fair to say that whenever a living trust is used, it can be wise to have either a pour-over to cover assets not transferred to the trust or a 'normal will'.

APPENDIX 1

LIVING TRUST WORKSHEET

LIVING TRUST WORKSHEET

www.enodare.com

LIVING TRUST WORKSHEET

Before you begin the process of making a living trust, we recommend that you print out this worksheet and complete it as appropriate. It will help you to work out what assets you actually own, and identify your liabilities, before deciding what assets you would like to transfer to your living trust and who you would like to make gifts to and how. By having all the relevant details at your fingertips it will save a considerable amount of time in the preparation of your living trust.

The document is also useful for documenting your choice of fiduciaries such as executors, trustees, healthcare agents etc.

In addition, by keeping this worksheet with your living trust, last will and other personal papers, it will greatly assist your trustees and executors in identifying and locating your assets and liabilities when the time comes.

Personal Information	You	Your Spouse
Full Name:		
Birth Date:		
Social Security Number:		
Occupation:		
Work Telephone:		
Work Fax:		
Mobile/Pager:		
Email Address:		
Home Address (Include County):		
Home Telephone:		

Home Fax:	
Date and Place of Marriage:	
Maiden name of spouse:	
If either of you were previously married, list the dates of prior marriage, name of previous spouse, names of living children from prior marriage(s), and state whether marriage ended by death or divorce:	
Location of Safe Deposit Box (if any):	

Notification of Death

(On my death, please notify the following persons)

Full Name	Telephone	Address

Children (Living)

Full Name	Address (If child does not reside with you)	Birth Date

Children (Deceased)

Full Name		

Grandchildren

Full Name	Address	Birth Date

Parents

Full Name	Address	Telephone Number

Brothers and Sisters

Full Name	Address	Telephone Number

Assets

Description & Location	Current Fair Market Value	How is Title Held?
Real Estate (Land and Buildings)		
Closely Held Companies, Businesses, Partnerships etc.		

Bank Accounts		
Shares, Bonds and Mutual Funds		
Vehicles, Boats, etc		

Other Property		
Total		

Liabilities

Description	Amount
Mortgages	
Loans	
Debts	
Other Liabilities	

Total	

Life Insurance and Annuities

Company	Insured	Beneficiary(ies)	Face Amount	Cash Value
Total				

Pensions and Other Retirement Plans

Company Custodian	Participant	Type of Plan	Vested Amount	Death Benefit

Total				

Distribution Plan
(Describe in general terms how you wish to leave your property at death)

Other Beneficiaries

(Information about persons other than your spouse and family members who you wish to benefit)

Full Name	Age	Address	Relationship to You

Fiduciaries

(List name, address and home telephone for each person)

	Full Name	Address	Telephone Number
Last Will and Testament			
Primary Executor			
First Alternate Executor			
Second Alternate Executor			
Primary Trustee			
First Alternate Trustee			
Second Alternate Trustee			

Guardian of Minor Children			
First Alternate Guardian			
Second Alternate Guardian			
Living Trust			
Successor Trustee			
First Alternate Successor Trustee			
Second Alternate Successor Trustee			
Agent under a Power of Attorney for Finance and Property (Durable Power of Attorney)			
Agent			
First Alternate Agent			
Second Alternate Agent			
Agent under a Healthcare Power of Attorney			
Healthcare Agent			
First Alternate Healthcare Agent			
Second Alternate Healthcare Agent			
Living Will			
Healthcare Agent			
First Alternate Healthcare Agent			
Second Alternate Healthcare Agent			

Advisors
(List name, address and home telephone for each person)

	Full Name	Address	Telephone Number
Lawyer			
Accountant			
Financial Advisor			
Stockbroker			
Insurance Agent			
Other Information:			

Document Locations

Description	Location	Other Information
Last Will & Testament		
Trust Agreement		
Living Will		
Healthcare Power of Attorney		
Power of Attorney for Finance and Property		
Title Deeds		
Leases		
Share Certificates		
Mortgage Documents		

Birth Certificate		
Marriage Certificate		
Divorce Decree		
Donor Cards		
Other Documents		

Funeral Plan
(Describe in general terms what funeral and burial arrangements you would like to have)

APPENDIX 2

INSTRUCTIONS FOR COMPLETING
YOUR DOCUMENTS

Revocable Living Trust for an Individual

1. On the cover page, insert the date of execution of the Agreement as well as your name as both grantor and trustee in the spaces provided. Remember, as you will act as both grantor and trustee, the agreement will be between you (as grantor) and you (as trustee).

2. On page 1, enter the date of execution of the Agreement at the very top of the Agreement.

3. The top half of page one identifies the parties to the agreement. You should enter your name and address in the spaces provided for insertion in (1) and (2) (details of both the grantor and trustee respectively).

4. At clause 1.1, insert details of the name of the trust. For example, if your name is John Smith, it is common to name the trust as "the John Smith Revocable Living Trust". Adopting this approach, just enter your name in the space provided.

5. In clause 4, you will instruct your successor trustee as to what gifts should be made and to whom on your death. In this clause, there are two types of gifts – specific gifts and gifts of the residuary trust estate.

Specific Gifts

You are not obliged to make any specific gifts. In fact, you can have as many specific gifts as you like or even none at all – the choice is yours. Depending on your preference in this respect, you will need to add or delete specific gift clauses from your agreement but remember to adjust the numbering in the clause accordingly.

To complete a standard gift clause, simply insert the name and address of the beneficiary into the gift clause together with details of what that beneficiary is to receive from the trust estate. If you wish to appoint an alternate beneficiary who will receive this gift if the primary beneficiary dies before you, you can do so. Simply, refer to Appendix 4 for an appropriate clause which can be substituted for the default clause in the agreement. Remember, there is no obligation on you to appoint an alternate beneficiary for a specific gift. If the primary beneficiary dies before you, and no alternate beneficiary is appointed the asset gifted to him/her under the agreement will revert to form part of the residuary trust estate.

Residuary Trust Estate

You must complete the gift of the residuary estate in all circumstances.

You can name one primary beneficiary and one or more alternates OR multiple primary beneficiaries and multiple alternates. The clause for a single primary beneficiary and a single alternate beneficiary is included by default in this agreement. If you wish to change this to multiple primary beneficiaries and/or multiple alternate beneficiaries, simply replace the default clause in the agreement with the relevant clause from Appendix 4.

To complete the residuary gift clause for a single primary beneficiary and single alternate beneficiary, simply insert the name and address of both the primary beneficiary and the alternate beneficiary in the spaces provided.

You can complete the residuary gift clause for multiple primary beneficiaries and multiple alternate beneficiaries in the same way as mentioned in the previous paragraph. However, in addition to the above, you will also need to specify what percentage of the overall trust estate each primary beneficiary is to receive. The total must of course equal 100%. Also, you must specify what percentage of the primary beneficiary's interest each alternate beneficiary is to receive. Remember, that the alternates should be allocated 100% of the primary beneficiary's interest of the trust estate.

<u>Simple Note:</u> Primary beneficiaries receive a % interest in the trust estate. They must be allocated 100% in total between them.

Alternate beneficiaries receive a % <u>interest in the primary beneficiary's share</u> of the trust estate...not an interest in the trust estate directly. 100% of the primary beneficiary's share should be divided between the alternates.

<u>Example:</u> (i) 20% thereof shall be given to Primary Beneficiary No 1 of Small Town, Big County, New York. In the event that the aforementioned person shall fail to survive the Grantor, his/her share of the Residue Trust Estate shall be given to Alternate Beneficiary No 1 of Small Town, Big County, New York.

<u>Example:</u> (ii) 20% thereof shall be given to Primary Beneficiary No 2 of Small Town, Big County, New York. In the event that the aforementioned person shall fail to survive the Grantor, his/her share of the Residue Trust Estate shall be divided by the Successor Trustee as follows:

i 60% thereof shall be given to Alternate Beneficiary No 2 of Small Town, Big County, New York.

       ii   40% thereof shall be given to Alternate Beneficiary No 3 of Small Town, Big County, New York.

6. In clause 7.1, insert the name and address of both your successor trustee and your alternate successor trustee.

7. At clause, 9.3 specify the state in which you are resident. The laws of this state will govern the operation of the trust.

8. On the execution page of the agreement, you should sign the agreement as both grantor and trustee in the presence of two witnesses. Your witnesses should each write their names and sign their names in the spaces provided.

9. In the schedule, you should insert details of all of the assets you are transferring to your revocable living trust. Remember, if the assets have title documents and a prescribed means by which they should be transferred, you should ensure that the transfer is carried out correctly. If there is no prescribed transfer document, but the transfer document is required you can use the deed of assignment contained in this kit. If you are in any doubt as to what document should be used to effect the transfer, speak to an attorney.

   If no transfer document is required, simply add details of the asset in the schedule at the back of the agreement.

10. The final page of the agreement contains a notary affidavit. There is generally no requirement that you have a notary complete this affidavit. However, we recommend that you have it completed as it lessens the likelihood that your execution of the trust agreement could be challenged by others. Simply bring the agreement together with identification to a notary and he or she will be able to assist you with the rest.

Note: If you wish to add any property management provisions, see Appendix 4. The relevant clause should be added at clause 5 of the trust agreement.

Revocable Living Trust for a Couple

1. On the cover page, insert the date of execution of the Agreement as well as the names of both grantors and trustees in the spaces provided. Remember, as you and your spouse will act as both grantors and trustees, the agreement will be between you and your spouse (as grantors) and you and your spouse (as trustees).

2. On page 1, enter the date of execution of the Agreement at the very top of the

Agreement.

3.   The top half of page one identifies the parties to the agreement. You should enter your name and address and your spouse's name and address in the spaces provided in (1) and (2) (details of both the grantors and trustees respectively).

4.   At rectal A, enter the husband's name.

5.   At recital B, enter the wife's name.

6.   At recital C, enter the name of the husband and then the wife.

7.   At clause 1.1, insert details of the name of the trust. For example, if your name is John Smith and your wife is Mary Smith, it is common to name the trust as "the John and Mary Smith Revocable Living Trust".

8.   At clause 2.4(i), enter the husband's name.

9.   At clause 2.4(ii), enter the wife's name.

10. At clause 2.4(iii), enter the name of the husband and then the wife.

11. At clause 3.1.1(a), enter the husband's name.

12. At clause 3.1.1(b), enter the wife's name.

13. At clause 3.1.3(a), enter the husband's name.

14. At clause 3.1.3(b), enter the wife's name.

15. At 4.6.1, enter the husband's name in both spaces. Then specify what gifts you would like to make from the husband's share of the trust assets. Remember, the husband will own the assets in schedule 1 and have an interest in the assets in schedule 3.

There are three specific gift clauses in this section. Specific gifts of an asset, specific gifts of an interest in an asset and gifts of the residue of the husband's estate. We will discuss each in turn.

Husband's Specific Gifts of Assets (Schedule 1)

The husband is not obliged to make any specific gifts from his share of the trust estate.

In fact, he can have as many specific gifts as he likes or even none at all – the choice is his. Depending on the preference in this respect, you will need to add or delete specific gift clauses from your agreement but remember to adjust the numbering in the clause accordingly.

To complete a standard gift clause, simply insert the name and address of the beneficiary into the gift clause together with details of what that beneficiary is to receive from the husband's trust estate. If you wish to appoint an alternate beneficiary who will receive this gift if the primary beneficiary dies before the husband, you can do so. Simply, refer to Appendix 4 for an appropriate clause which can be substituted for the default clause in this agreement. Remember, there is no obligation to appoint an alternate beneficiary for a specific gift. If the primary beneficiary dies before the husband, and no alternate beneficiary is appointed, the asset gifted to him/her under the agreement will revert to form part of the husband's residuary trust estate.

Husband's Specific Gifts of an Interest in Assets (Schedule 3)

This clause is completed in much the same way as a specific gift of an asset and it too can contain provisions for an alternate beneficiary. The only addition is that, in completing the clause, the husband's name must be entered into the clause after the name and address of the beneficiary and before the details of the relevant asset. See the example below for an illustration:-

(i) [Primary Beneficiary Name] of [Primary Beneficiary Address] shall be given [Husband's Name]'s interest in [Details of Asset].

Gift of Husbands Residuary Estate

You must complete the gift of the husband's residuary trust estate in all circumstances. You can name one primary beneficiary and one or more alternate beneficiaries OR multiple primary beneficiaries and multiple alternates. The clause for a single primary beneficiary and a single alternate beneficiary is included by default in this agreement. If you wish to change this to multiple primary beneficiaries and/or multiple alternate beneficiaries, simply replace the default clause in the agreement with the relevant clause from Appendix 4.

To complete the residuary gift clause for a single primary beneficiary and single alternate beneficiary, simply insert the name and address of both the primary beneficiary and the alternate beneficiary in the spaces provided. You will also need to insert the husband's name in the relevant places. See completed example below:-

(i)   Any of [Husband Name]'s Trust Estate not otherwise disposed of hereunder ("[Husband Name]'s Residue Trust Estate") shall be given to [Primary Beneficiary Name] of [Primary Beneficiary Address] for his/her own use and benefit absolutely. If the aforementioned person predeceases [Husband Name] then in that event his/her share of [Husband Name]'s Residue Trust Estate shall be given to [Alternate Beneficiary Name] of [Alternate Beneficiary Address].

You can complete the residuary gift clause for multiple primary beneficiaries and multiple alternate beneficiaries in the same way as mentioned in the previous paragraph. However, in addition to the above, you will also need to specify what percentage of the husband's overall trust estate each primary beneficiary is to receive. The total must of course equal 100%. Also, you must specify what percentage of the primary beneficiary's interest each alternate beneficiary is to receive. Remember, that the alternates should be allocated 100% of the primary beneficiary's interest in the husband's trust estate.

Simple Note: Primary beneficiaries receive a % interest in the husband's trust estate. They must be allocated 100% in total between them.

Alternate beneficiaries receive a % interest in the primary beneficiaries' share of the husband's trust estate...not an interest in the husband's trust estate directly. 100% of the primary beneficiary's share should be divided between the alternates.

Example: Any of [Husband Name]'s Trust Estate not otherwise disposed of hereunder ("[Husband Name]'s Residue Trust Estate") shall be divided by the Successor Trustee as follows:

(i)   20% thereof shall be given to [Primary Beneficiary 1 Name] of [Primary Beneficiary 1 Address]. In the event that the aforementioned person shall fail to survive [Husband Name], his/her share of [Husband Name]'s Residue Trust Estate shall be divided by the Successor Trustee as follows:

i   60% thereof shall be given to [Alternate Beneficiary 1 Name] of [Alternate Beneficiary 1 Address].

ii   40% thereof shall be given to [Alternate Beneficiary 2 Name] of [Alternate Beneficiary 2 Address].

(ii)   80% thereof shall be given to [Primary Beneficiary 2 Name] of [Primary Beneficiary 2 Address]. In the event that the aforementioned person shall fail to survive [Husband Name], his/her share of [Husband Name]'s Residue Trust Estate shall be divided by the Successor Trustee as follows:

    i   50% thereof shall be given to [Alternate Beneficiary 3 Name] of [Alternate Beneficiary 3 Address].

    ii   50% thereof shall be given to [Alternate Beneficiary 3 Name] of [Alternate Beneficiary 3 Address].

16. Clause 4.6.2, the wife's gifts, should be completed in a manner similar to that set out at point 15 above in respect of the distribution of the husband's gifts. Of course, the wife is free to choose her own beneficiaries. The reference to husband should be considered to be to wife and the reference to Schedule 1 should be considered to be Schedule 2.

17. In clause 8.1, insert the name and address of both your successor trustee and your alternate successor trustee.

18. At clause 10.3, specify the state in which you are resident. The laws of this state will govern the operation of the trust.

19. On the execution page of the agreement, both the husband and wife should sign the agreement as both grantor and trustee in the presence of two witnesses. Both husband and wife will therefore each need to sign twice. Your witness should each write their names and sign their names in the spaces provided.

20. In the schedules, you should insert details of all of the assets being transferred to the revocable living trust. Details of the husband's solely owned assets should be included in Schedule 1. Details of the wife's solely owned assets should be included in Schedule 2. Details of the assets owned jointly by both spouses should be included in Schedule 3.

Remember, if the assets have title documents and a prescribed means by which they should be transferred, you should ensure that the transfer is carried out correctly. If there is no prescribed transfer document but a transfer document is required, you can use the deed of assignment contained at the back of this kit. If you are in any doubt as to what document should be used to effect the transfer, speak to an attorney.

21. The final page of the agreement contains a notary affidavit. There is generally no requirement that you have a notary complete this affidavit. However, we recommend that you have it completed as it lessens the likelihood that the execution of the trust agreement could be challenged by others. Simply bring the agreement together with identification to a notary and he or she will be able to assist you with the rest. Both you and your spouse should attend.

Note: If you wish to add any property management provisions, see Appendix 4. The relevant clause should be added at clause 5 of the trust agreement.

Deed of Assignment for Use with a Revocable Living Trust for an Individual

1. On the cover page, insert the date of execution of the deed as well as your name as both grantor and trustee in the spaces provided. Remember, as you are acting as both grantor and trustee, the deed will be between you (as grantor) and you (as trustee).

2. On page 1, enter the date of execution of the deed at the very top of the page.

3. The top half of page one identifies the parties to the deed. You should enter your name and address in the spaces provided for insertion in (1) and (2) (details of both the grantor and trustee respectively).

4. In Recital A, enter the date of creation of the trust and the name of the trust.

5. At clause 1.1, insert details of the assets you wish to transfer by deed of assignment to the trust. Remember to be as specific as possible in describing the assets.

6. Print your name in the execution block on the last page and sign your name directly opposite the execution block in the space provided. You should sign your name in the presence of a witness. The witness should print and sign his/her name in the spaces provided under your execution block.

Deed of Assignment for Use with a Revocable Living Trust for a Couple

1. On the cover page, insert the date of execution of the deed as well as your name and that of your spouse as both grantors and trustees in the spaces provided. Remember, as

you and your spouse are grantors and trustees, the deed will be between you and your spouse (as grantors) and you and your spouse (as trustees).

2. On page 1, enter the date of execution of the deed at the very top of the page.

3. The top half of page one identifies the parties to the deed. You should enter your name and address and your spouse's name and address in the spaces provided for insertion in (1) and (2) (details of both the grantors and trustees respectively).

4. In Recital A, enter the date of creation of the trust and the name of the trust.

5. At clause 1.1, insert details of the assets you wish to transfer by deed of assignment to the trust. Remember to be as specific as possible in describing the assets. You can include both solely owned assets and jointly owned assets in this section.

6. Print your name in the execution block on the last page and sign your name directly opposite the execution block in the space provided. You should sign your name in the presence of a witness. The witness should print and sign his/her name in the spaces provided under your execution block. You should repeat the process for your spouse.

Notice of Revocation

1. On the cover page, insert the date of execution of the notice of revocation as well as your name as grantor in the spaces provided.

2. On page 1, enter your name and address, the date the trust was established and the date of execution of the notice of revocation. Sign your name as grantor in the space provided.

3. The final page of the agreement contains a notary affidavit. There is generally no requirement that you have a notary complete this affidavit. However, we recommend that you have it completed as it lessens the likelihood that your execution of the notice of revocation could be challenged by others. Simply bring the notice together with identification to a notary and he or she will be able to assist you with the rest.

4. The notice should be sent to all trustees of the trust (including you).

APPENDIX 3

REVOCABLE LIVING TRUST DOCUMENTS

CD-ROM & Downloadable Forms

Blank copies of all of the forms contained in this book are available on the CD-ROM which accompanies this book. Alternatively all forms can be downloaded from the enodare website.

Web: http://www.enodare.com/downloadarea/

Unlock Code: LVT35627

REVOCABLE LIVING TRUST AGREEMENT FOR AN INDIVIDUAL

DATED THIS ____ DAY OF _____, 20___.

_____
(Grantor)

and

_____
(Trustee)

REVOCABLE LIVING TRUST AGREEMENT

www.enodare.com

REVOCABLE LIVING TRUST AGREEMENT

AGREEMENT made this _____ day of _____, 20___.

BETWEEN:

(1) _____ of _____ (the "**Grantor**"), and

(2) _____ of _____ (the "**Trustee**").

WHEREAS:

A.   The Grantor is the legal and beneficial owner of the property described in the Schedule attached hereto.

B.   The Grantor wishes to create a trust of certain property for the grantor's benefit and for the benefit of others, such property being described in the Schedule attached hereto and having been delivered this date to the Trustee of the trust created hereunder.

C.   The Grantor may wish to add other property to the trust at a later date by gift, devise or bequest under the terms of a Last Will and Testament or otherwise by depositing such other property with the Trustee (or with any Successor Trustee).

D.   The Trustee is willing and hereby agrees to perform the duties of trustee in accordance with the terms and conditions and within the powers and limitations set out in this Agreement.

IT IS AGREED AS FOLLOWS:

In consideration of the mutual covenants set forth herein, and for other good and valuable consideration (receipt of which is hereby acknowledged), the Grantor and Trustee hereby agree as follows:

1.   **NAME OF THE TRUST**

1.1   This trust shall be designated as the _____ Revocable Living Trust (the "Trust").

2.   TRANSFER OF PROPERTY

2.1   The Grantor, in consideration of the acceptance by the Trustee of the trust herein created, hereby conveys, transfers, assigns, and delivers to the Trustee the property described in the Schedule hereto (the "Trust Estate") to hold same on trust for the uses and purposes set out below and in accordance with the terms of this Agreement.

2.2   The Grantor, and any other persons, shall have the right at any time to add property acceptable to the Trustee to the Trust and such property, when received and accepted by the Trustee, shall become a part of the Trust Estate and shall be noted in the Schedule hereto.

2.3   Notwithstanding any other provision of this Agreement, if the Grantor's principal place of residence forms part of the Trust Estate, the Grantor hereby reserves the right to possess, occupy and enjoy such premises and its surrounds for life, rent-free and without charge save for any taxes and other expenses properly payable by the Grantor.

3.   DISPOSITION OF INCOME AND PRINCIPAL DURING THE LIFETIME OF THE GRANTOR

3.1   The Trustee shall manage, invest and hold the Trust Estate and collect the income derived therefrom and, after the payment of all taxes and assessments thereon and all charges incident to the management thereof, dispose of the net income therefrom and corpus thereof, as follows:

3.1.1   During the lifetime of the Grantor, the Trustee shall pay the income arising to the Trust Estate, together with such portions of the principal as the Grantor may from time to time direct, to the Grantor or otherwise as the Grantor may from time to time direct during the Grantor's life.

3.1.2   During the lifetime of the Grantor, the Trustee may pay to or apply for the benefit of the Grantor such sums from the principal of the Trust as the Trustee shall in his or her absolute discretion consider necessary or advisable from time to time for the medical care, comfortable maintenance and welfare of the Grantor, taking into consideration any other income or resources of the Grantor known to the Trustee.

3.1.3   The Grantor may at any time during the Grantor's lifetime and from time to time, withdraw all or part of the principal of the Trust, free of trust, by delivering to the Trustee an instrument in writing duly signed by the Grantor describing the property or portion thereof to be withdrawn. Upon receipt of such instrument, the Trustee shall thereupon convey, assign, deliver and execute any document necessary and do every act or thing necessary to transfer to the Grantor, free from the provisions of this Trust, the property described in the said instrument.

3.1.4 In the event that the Grantor is deemed to be mentally incompetent (as determined in writing by a qualified medical doctor) and unable to manage his or her own affairs, or in the event that the Grantor is not adjudicated incompetent, but by reason of illness or mental or physical disability is, in the reasonable opinion of the Successor Trustee, unable to properly handle his or her own affairs, then and in that event the Successor Trustee may during the Grantor's lifetime, in addition to the payments of income and principal for the benefit of the Grantor (including the medical care, comfortable maintenance and welfare of the Grantor), pay to or apply for the benefit of the Grantor's minor children and other dependents (if any), such sums from the net income and from the principal of this Trust in such shares and proportions as the Successor Trustee determines to be necessary or advisable from time to time for the medical care, comfortable maintenance and welfare of the Grantor's minor children and dependents taking into consideration, to the extent the Successor Trustee deems fit, any other income or resources of the Grantor's minor children and dependents known to the Successor Trustee.

3.1.5 The interests of the Grantor shall at all times be considered primary and superior to the interests of any beneficiary hereunder.

4. DISTRIBUTION OF TRUST ESTATE FOLLOWING THE DEATH OF THE GRANTOR

4.1 After the death of the Grantor, the Successor Trustee shall promptly distribute the Trust Estate to the following persons (the "Beneficiaries") as follows:

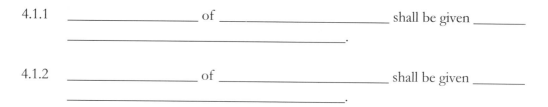

4.1.1 _____ of _____ shall be given _____
_____.

4.1.2 _____ of _____ shall be given _____
_____.

[Repeat or delete as necessary to make further specific gifts. Note you may need to renumber subsequent clauses]

4.1.3 Any of the Trust Estate not otherwise disposed of hereunder (the

"Residue Trust Estate") shall be given to _____ of
_____ for his/her own use and benefit absolutely. If the
aforementioned person predeceases the Grantor or refuses to accept the gift
then, in that event, his/her share of the Residue Trust Estate shall be given to
_____ of _____.

## 5.	PROPERTY MANAGEMENT

5.1	The Successor Trustee shall be entitled (but shall not be obliged) to transfer the share
of any minor Beneficiary for whom alternative property management provisions have
not otherwise been made herein to the legal guardian or custodian of the Beneficiary
upon production of such evidence by the said guardian or custodian to establish to
the reasonable satisfaction of the Successor Trustee that such person stands as legal
guardian or custodian to the said Beneficiary. Any such transfer shall be a good discharge
of the Successor Trustee's obligations in that respect.

5.2	If any Beneficiary for whom a share is held in trust should die before having received all
the principal and income thereof, then upon his or her death the remaining principal and
income shall be paid to his or her then living child or children, equally if more than one,
and in default thereof, to the residuary beneficiary named herein, and if more than one
residuary beneficiary, in equal shares absolutely.

## 6.	POWERS OF TRUSTEES

6.1	In addition to any powers granted under applicable law or otherwise, and not in
limitation of such powers, but subject to any rights and powers which may be reserved
expressly by the Grantor in this Agreement, the Trustee and any Successor Trustee
validly acting hereunder (each a "trustee") shall have full power:

(i)	to hold and retain any and all property, real, personal, or mixed, received from
any other source for such time as the trustee shall deem fit, and to dispose of
such property by sale, exchange, assignment, lease, license or otherwise, as and
when the trustee shall deem fit;

(ii)	to sell, assign, exchange, transfer, partition, convey, license, lease, rent, hire, grant
options over or otherwise dispose of any property, real or personal, which forms
part of the Trust Estate, upon such terms and conditions and in such manner as
the trustee deems fit; and for that purpose to make, execute, acknowledge and
deliver any and all instruments, deeds and assignments in such form and with
such warranties and covenants as the trustee may deem fit;

(iii)   to lease, license, rent and manage any or all of the assets, real or personal, of the Trust Estate, upon such terms and conditions as the trustee in his/her absolute discretion deems fit; and for that purpose to make, execute, acknowledge and deliver any and all instruments, deeds and assignments in such form and with such warranties and covenants as the trustee may deem fit; and to make repairs, replacements, and improvements, structural and otherwise, to any property, and to charge the expense thereof in an equitable manner to the principal or income of the Trust Estate, as the trustee deems fit;

(iv)   to borrow money for any purpose in connection with the Trust, and to execute promissory notes or other obligations for amounts so borrowed, and to secure the payment of any such amounts by mortgage or pledge of any real or personal property, and to renew or extend the time of payment of any obligation, secured or unsecured, payable to or by any trust created hereby, for such periods of time as the trustee may deem fit;

(v)   to invest any or all of the funds of the Trust Estate in such manner as the trustee, acting in his/her absolute discretion, deems fit;

(vi)   to deal with the Trust Estate generally for the benefit of the Beneficiaries;

(vii)   to compromise, adjust, arbitrate, sue, institute, defend, abandon, settle or otherwise deal with proceedings of any kind on behalf of or against the Trust or the Trust Estate as the trustee shall in his/her sole and absolute discretion deem fit;

(viii)   to determine in a fair and reasonable manner whether any part of the Trust Estate, or any addition or increment thereto be income or principal, or whether any cost, charge, expense, tax, or assessment shall be charged against income or principal, or partially against income and partially against principal;

(ix)   to vote any stocks, shares, bonds, securities or any other voting rights held by the Trust or attributable to the Trust Estate; and to delegate such voting power in such manner as the trustee may deem fit having regard to any legal requirements;

(x)   to consent to the reorganization, consolidation, merger, liquidation, readjustment of, or other change in any corporation, company, or association and to execute such documents and do all such acts and things as may reasonably be required to effect same;

(xi)   to engage in business with the Trust Estate property as sole proprietor, or as a general or limited partner, with all the powers customarily exercised by an individual so engaged in business, and to hold an undivided interest in any property as tenant in common or as tenant in partnership, to the extent permitted by law; and to enter into such agreements and contracts as the trustee may deem necessary to regulate such businesses;

(xii) to purchase securities, real estate, or other property from any party connected to the Grantor, be it by contract or blood, provided such purchase is on an arm's length basis at market value and same is in the best interest of the Grantor and the Beneficiaries hereunder;

(xiii) to make loans or advancements to any party connected to the Grantor, be it by contract or blood, provided such loans or advancements are on an arm's length basis and in the best interest of the Grantors and the Beneficiaries hereunder;

(xiv) to act through an agent or attorney-in-fact, by and under a power of attorney duly executed by the trustee to the extent permitted by law, in carrying out any of the authorized powers and duties; and

(xv) to undertake such further acts as are incidental to any of the foregoing or are reasonably required to carry out the tenor, purpose and intent of the Trust.

6.2 The powers granted to the Trustee and Successor Trustee under Clause 6.1 may be exercised in whole or in part, from time to time, and shall be deemed to be supplementary to and not exclusive of the general powers of trustees pursuant to law, and shall include all powers necessary to carry them into effect.

6.3 Notwithstanding anything contained herein to the contrary, no powers enumerated or accorded to trustees generally pursuant to law shall be construed to enable the Grantor, or the Trustee or either of them, or any other person, to sell, purchase, exchange, or otherwise deal with or dispose of all or any part of the corpus or income of the trusts for less than an adequate consideration in money or money's worth, or to enable the Grantor to borrow all or any part of the corpus or income of the trusts, directly or indirectly, without adequate interest or security.

7.   SUCCESSOR TRUSTEE

7.1 In the event of the death or during any period of incapacity of the Trustee, _____ of _____ is hereby nominated and appointed as the successor trustee to the trustee (the "Successor Trustee"). In the event the aforementioned person is unable or unwilling to act as Successor Trustee,

_____ of _____ is hereby nominated and appointed as Successor Trustee.

7.2   If none of the persons named in Clause 7.1 are able and willing to act as successor trustee, then any of the nominated Successor Trustees may appoint (with preference going to the primary successor trustee's nomination) a replacement successor trustee to serve as Successor Trustee hereunder provided that such appointment is made in writing, signed by the Successor Trustee making the appointment, notarized and forwarded to each of the named Beneficiaries. In the event the that no Successor Trustee is willing and able to make such an appointment or in the event that the Successor Trustees fail to secure the appointment of a new Successor Trustee and notify the Beneficiaries of such appointment within 7 days of the declining Successor Trustee's refusal to act, then the next Successor Trustees shall be chosen by a majority in interest of the then living Beneficiaries, with a parent or guardian voting for each minor Beneficiary.

7.3   On acting, a Successor Trustee may, by notice in writing to the next Successor Trustee and to all Beneficiaries, resign from office at any time provided at least 14 days notice in writing of such resignation is provided. The resigning Successor Trustee shall prior to his or her resignation taking effect deliver an accounting of the assets, income and expenses of the Trust (and all sub-trusts, if any) to the next Successor Trustee. This accounting shall be made up to the date of resignation of the Successor Trustee. In the event of there being no readily identifiable Successor Trustee, the resigning Successor Trustee shall procure the appointment of a new Successor Trustee which may for the avoidance of doubt include a bank or trust company and shall notify the Beneficiaries in writing in the manner described in Clause 7.2 above. In the event that the Successor Trustee fails to secure the appointment of a new Successor Trustee and notify the Beneficiaries of same before the date of his or her resignation taking effect, then the next Successor Trustee shall be chosen by a majority in interest of the then living Beneficiaries, with a parent or guardian voting for each minor Beneficiary.

7.4   The appointment of the Successor Trustee(s) under this Clause shall automatically terminate at the end of any period in which the Grantor is incapacitated but such termination shall not impact the automatic re-appointment of such Successor Trustee(s) on the death of the Grantor or during any period of future incapacity of the Grantor, as contemplated by Clause 7.1.

7.5   A Successor Trustee shall (in his/her capacity as Successor Trustee) be able to exercise all the powers of the Trustee hereunder including, for the avoidance of doubt, but not limited to, the powers of the Trustee referred to in Clauses 3 to 6 hereof.

7.6   The Trustee and each Successor Trustee named herein (including any alternate named herein) shall serve without bond. A resigning Successor Trustee may require a bond to be posted by any other incoming Successor Trustee, the cost of such bond being payable from the Trust Estate. The Successor Trustee shall not be liable for any mistake or error of judgment in the administration of the Trust, except for willful misconduct, so long as he or she continue to exercise his or her duties and powers in a fiduciary capacity primarily in the interests of the Beneficiaries.

8.   **REVOCATION AND AMENDMENT**

8.1   The Grantor shall have the irrevocable right to and may by instrument in writing signed by the Grantor and delivered to the Trustee, revoke, modify or alter this Agreement, in whole or in part, without the consent of the Trustee or any Beneficiary. Save as may otherwise be provided herein, the Trust shall not be amended, modified, revoked or terminated in any other way.

9.   **ADMINISTRATIVE PROVISIONS**

9.1   The Trustee may at his or her absolute discretion, but shall not be obliged to, render an accounting at any time.

9.2   The Trustee hereby waives the payment of any compensation for his or her services, but this waiver shall not apply to any Successor Trustee who qualifies and acts under this Agreement and who shall be entitled to reasonable compensation for his or her service.

9.3   This Trust has been accepted by the Trustee and will be administered in the State of _____ and its validity, construction, and all rights hereunder shall be governed by the laws of that State and that State shall have exclusive jurisdiction to determine any disputes which may arise hereunder.

IN WITNESS WHEREOF, the Grantor and Trustee have executed this Agreement on the date above written.

_____

Signature of Grantor

_____

Signature of Trustee

_____   _____

Name of First Witness   Signature of First Witness

_____   _____
Name of Second Witness   Signature of Second Witness

SCHEDULE

_____
_____
_____
_____
_____
_____
_____
_____
_____
_____
_____
_____
_____
_____
_____
_____
_____
_____
_____
_____
_____
_____
_____
_____
_____
_____
_____
_____
_____
_____

NOTARY AFFIDAVIT

STATE OF _____   **COUNTY OF** _____

On _____ before me, _____, a notary public, personally appeared _____, who proved to me on the basis of satisfactory evidence to be the person whose name is subscribed to the within instrument and acknowledged to me that he/she executed the same in his/her authorized capacity, and that by his/her signature on the instrument the person executed the instrument. I certify under PENALTY OF PERJURY that the foregoing is true and correct. Witness my hand and official seal.

Signature: _____
Print Name: _____
My commission expires on: _____
(Seal)

REVOCABLE LIVING TRUST AGREEMENT
FOR A COUPLE

DATED THIS ____ DAY OF _____, 20___.

_____ **AND** _____
(Grantors)

and

_____ **AND** _____
(Trustees)

REVOCABLE LIVING TRUST AGREEMENT

www.enodare.com

REVOCABLE LIVING TRUST AGREEMENT

AGREEMENT made this _____ day of _____, 20___.

BETWEEN:

(1) _____ of _____ and _____ of _____ (hereinafter referred to jointly as the "Grantors"), and

(2) _____ of _____ and _____ of _____ (hereinafter referred to jointly as the "Trustees").

WHEREAS:

A. _____ is the legal and beneficial owner of the property described in Schedule One attached hereto.

B. _____ is the legal and beneficial owner of the property described in Schedule Two attached hereto.

C. Each of _____ and _____ jointly own the property described in Schedule Three.

D. The Grantors wish to create a trust of certain property for the benefit of themselves and others, such property being described in Schedules One, Two and Three attached hereto and having been delivered this date to the Trustees of the trust created hereunder.

E. The Grantors may wish to add other property to the trust at a later date by gift, devise or bequest under the terms of a Last Will and Testament or otherwise by depositing such other property with any Trustee (or with any Successor Trustee).

F. The Trustees are willing and hereby agree to perform the duties of trustee in accordance with the terms and conditions and within the powers and limitations set out in this Agreement.

IT IS AGREED AS FOLLOWS:

In consideration of the mutual covenants set forth herein, and for other good and valuable consideration (receipt of which is hereby acknowledged), the Grantors and Trustees hereby agree as follows:

1.   **NAME OF THE TRUST**

1.1   This trust shall be designated as the _____ Revocable Living Trust
        (the "Trust").

2.   **TRANSFER OF PROPERTY**

2.1   The Grantors, in consideration of the acceptance by the Trustees of the trust herein
        created, hereby jointly and severally convey, transfer, assign, and deliver to the Trustees
        the property described in Schedules One, Two and Three hereto (the "Trust Estate") to
        hold same on trust for the uses and purposes set out below and in accordance with the
        terms of this Agreement.

2.2   The Grantors, and any other persons, shall have the right at any time to add property
        acceptable to the Trustees (or the survivor of them) to the Trust and such property,
        when received and accepted by the Trustees (or the survivor of them), shall become
        a part of the Trust Estate and shall be held in accordance with the terms of this
        Agreement, in particular Clause 2.4, and shall be noted accordingly in the relevant
        Schedule hereto.

2.3   Notwithstanding any other provision of this Agreement, if the Grantors' principal place
        of residence forms part of the Trust Estate, the Grantors hereby reserve the right to
        possess, occupy and enjoy such premises and its surrounds for life without fee or charge
        save that they shall be accountable for any taxes and other expenses properly payable by
        them in respect of such property.

2.4   For so long as both Grantors remain alive:

        (a)   _____ shall retain all control of and rights to all income and profits
                derived from the assets of the Trust Estate described in Schedule One;

        (b)   _____ shall retain all control of and rights to all income and profits
                derived from the assets of the Trust Estate described in Schedule Two; and

        (c)   _____ and _____ shall respectively retain all
                control over and all rights to income and profits derived from their respective assets
                (or share thereof) of the Trust Estate described in Schedule Three.

3.   **DISPOSITION OF INCOME AND PRINCIPAL DURING THE LIFE OF
        THE GRANTORS**

3.1   The Trustees shall manage, invest and hold the Trust Estate and collect the income derived therefrom and, after the payment of all taxes and assessments thereon and all charges incident to the management thereof, dispose of the net income therefrom and corpus thereof, as follows:

    3.1.1   For so long as both Grantors shall be living, the Trustees shall pay to:

        (a)   _____ (or as he may otherwise direct) the income arising to that part of the Trust Estate described in Schedule One, together with such portions of the related principal as he may from time to time direct;

        (b)   _____ (or as she may otherwise direct) the income arising to that part of the Trust Estate described in Schedule Two, together with such portions of the related principal as she may from time to time direct; and

        (c)   the Grantors (jointly) (or as they may otherwise jointly direct in writing) the income arising to that part of the Trust Estate described in Schedule Three, together with such portions of the related principal as they may from time to time direct in writing.

    3.1.2   During the lifetime of the Grantors, the Trustees may pay to or apply for the benefit of the Grantors such sums from the principal of the Trust as the Trustees shall in their absolute discretion consider necessary or advisable from time to time for the medical care, comfortable maintenance and welfare of the Grantors, taking into consideration any other income or resources of the Grantors known to the Trustees.

    3.1.3

        (a)   _____ may at any time withdraw all or part of the principal of the Trust Estate described in Schedule One (free of trust) by delivering to the Trustees an instrument in writing duly signed by him.

        (b)   _____ may at any time withdraw all or part of the principal of the Trust Estate described in Schedule Two (free of trust) by delivering to the Trustees an instrument in writing duly signed by her.

        (c)   The Grantors, acting jointly, may at any time withdraw all or part of the principal of the Trust Estate described in Schedule Three (free of trust) by delivering to the Trustees an instrument in writing duly signed by each of them. Upon receipt of such instrument, the Trustees shall thereupon convey, assign, deliver and execute any document necessary and do every act or thing necessary to transfer to the Grantors, or either of them as the case may be, free from the provisions of this Trust, the property described in the said instrument.

3.1.4 In the event that both the Grantors are deemed to be mentally incompetent (as determined in writing by a qualified medical doctor) and unable to manage their own affairs, or in the event that the Grantors are not adjudicated incompetent, but by reason of illness or mental or physical disability are, in the reasonable opinion of the Successor Trustee, unable to properly handle their own affairs, then and in that event the Successor Trustee may during the Grantors' lifetimes, in addition to the payments of income and principal for the benefit of the Grantors, pay to or apply for the benefit of the Grantors' minor children and other dependents (if any), such sums from the net income and from the principal of this Trust in such shares and proportions as the Successor Trustee shall determine to be necessary or advisable from time to time for the medical care, comfortable maintenance and welfare of the Grantors' minor children and dependents taking into consideration, to the extent the Successor Trustee deems fit, any other income or resources of the Grantors' minor children and dependents known to the Successor Trustee.

3.1.5 The interests of the Grantors shall at all times be considered primary and superior to the interests of any beneficiary hereunder.

4. DIVISION AND DISTRIBUTION OF TRUST ESTATE FOLLOWING THE DEATH OF A GRANTOR

4.1 Immediately upon the death of a Grantor (the "Deceased Grantor"), the Trust shall hereby be deemed to automatically divide into two separate trusts, to be known as the First Trust and the Second Trust, each of which is to be governed in the manner set out herein and the surviving Grantor (the "Surviving Grantor") shall serve as trustee of each such trust.

4.2 Subject to Clause 4.3, the First Trust shall be deemed to and shall hereby include (i) all the Trust Estate owned by the Deceased Grantor immediately prior to its transfer to the Trust (ii) plus the Deceased Grantor's share of the Trust Estate described in Schedule Three as at the date of death of the Deceased Grantor (iii) plus any related accumulated income, appreciation in value or assets represented thereby or derived therefrom and attributable to the ownership by the Deceased Grantor of the Trust Estate. The remainder of the Trust Estate shall vest in the Second Trust.

4.3   Any property of the Trust Estate gifted by the Deceased Grantor to the Surviving Grantor shall remain in the Second Trust.

4.4   The First Trust shall be irrevocable from inception. The Second Trust shall be revocable from inception but shall become irrevocable on the death of the Surviving Grantor.

4.5   Save in respect of any gifts made by the Deceased Grantor to the Surviving Grantor, the surviving Trustee shall distribute the property contained in the First Trust in accordance with the provisions of Clause 4.6 below.

4.6

    4.6.1   On the death of _____, the Trust Estate described in Schedule One and _____'s share of the Trust Estate described in Schedule Three shall be promptly distributed to the following persons (the "Beneficiaries") as follows:

        (i)   _____ of _____ shall be given _____.

        (ii)   _____ of _____ shall be given _____.

        [Repeat or delete as necessary to make further specific gifts. Note you may need to renumber subsequent clauses]

        (iii)   _____ of _____ shall be given _____'s interest in _____ _____.

        (iv)   _____ of _____ shall be given _____'s interest in _____ _____.

        [Repeat or delete as necessary to make further specific gifts. Note you may need to renumber subsequent clauses]

        (v)   Any of _____'s Trust Estate not otherwise disposed of hereunder ("_____'s Residue Trust Estate") shall be given to _____ of _____ for his/her own use and benefit absolutely. If the aforementioned person predeceases _____ or refuses to accept this gift then in that event his/her share of _____'s Residue Trust Estate shall be given to _____ of _____.

4.6.2   On the death of _____, the Trust Estate described in Schedule Two and _____'s share of the Trust Estate described in Schedule Three shall be promptly distributed to the following persons (also the "Beneficiaries") as follows:

(i)   _____ of _____ shall be given _____.

(ii)   _____ of _____ shall be given _____.

[Repeat or delete as necessary to make further specific gifts. Note you may need to renumber subsequent clauses]

(iii)   _____ of _____ shall be given _____'s interest in _____ _____.

(iv)   _____ of _____ shall be given _____'s interest in _____ _____.

[Repeat or delete as necessary to make further specific gifts. Note you may need to renumber subsequent clauses]

(v)   Any of _____'s Trust Estate not otherwise disposed of hereunder ("_____'s Residue Trust Estate") shall be given to _____ of _____ for his/her own use and benefit absolutely. If the aforementioned person predeceases _____ or refuses to accept this gift then in that event his/her share of _____'s Residue Trust Estate shall be given to _____ of _____.

4.7   If both Grantors die in circumstances which make it difficult or impossible to determine who predeceased the other, then for the purpose of this Agreement it shall be conclusively presumed that both died at the same moment and that neither survived the other. In such circumstances, the Successor Trustee shall distribute the Trust Estate in accordance with the wishes of each Grantor as described in Clause 4.6 above.

5. PROPERTY MANAGEMENT

5.1 The Successor Trustee or surviving Trustee, as the case may be, shall be entitled (but shall not be obliged) to transfer the share of any minor Beneficiary for whom alternative property management provisions have not otherwise been made herein to the legal guardian or custodian of the Beneficiary upon production of such evidence by the said guardian or custodian to establish to the reasonable satisfaction of the Successor Trustee or surviving Trustee, as the case may be, that such person stands as legal guardian or custodian to the said Beneficiary. Any such transfer shall be a good discharge of the Surviving Trustee's or the Successor Trustee's obligations in that respect.

5.2 If any Beneficiary for whom a share is held in trust should die before having received all the principal and income thereof, then upon his or her death the remaining principal and income shall be paid to his or her then living child or children, equally if more than one, and in default thereof, to the residuary beneficiary of the gifting Grantor named herein, and if more than one residuary beneficiary, in equal shares absolutely.

6. ADMINISTRATION OF THE SECOND TRUST

6.1 The Second Trust shall be administered for the benefit of the Surviving Grantor in the manner described at Clause 3 above and the Trustee of the Second Trust shall have all of the rights referred to therein as well as any other rights of Trustees hereunder.

6.2 Upon the death of the Surviving Grantor, the Trust property contained in the Second Trust shall be distributed to the beneficiaries of the Surviving Grantor in the manner set out in Clause 4.6 above.

7. POWERS OF TRUSTEES

7.1 In addition to any powers granted under applicable law or otherwise, and not in limitation of such powers, but subject to any rights and powers which may be reserved expressly by the Grantors in this Agreement, the Trustees appointed hereunder shall have full power:

    (i)   to hold and retain any and all property, real, personal, or mixed, received from any other source for such time as the Trustees shall deem fit, and to dispose of such property by sale, exchange, assignment, lease, license or otherwise, as and when they shall deem fit;

(ii) to sell, assign, exchange, transfer, partition, convey, license, lease, rent, hire, grant options over or otherwise dispose of any property, real or personal, which forms part of the Trust Estate, upon such terms and conditions and in such manner as the Trustees deem fit; and for that purpose to make, execute, acknowledge and deliver any and all instruments, deeds and assignments in such form and with such warranties and covenants as the Trustees may deem fit;

(ii) to lease, license, rent and manage any or all of the assets, real or personal, of the Trust Estate, upon such terms and conditions as the Trustees in their absolute discretion deem fit; and for that purpose to make, execute, acknowledge and deliver any and all instruments, deeds and assignments in such form and with such warranties and covenants as the Trustees may deem fit; and to make repairs, replacements, and improvements, structural and otherwise, to any property, and to charge the expense thereof in an equitable manner to the principal or income of the Trust Estate, as the Trustees deem fit;

(iii) to borrow money for any purpose in connection with the Trust, and to execute promissory notes or other obligations for amounts so borrowed, and to secure the payment of any such amounts by mortgage or pledge of any real or personal property, and to renew or extend the time of payment of any obligation, secured or unsecured, payable to or by any trust created hereby, for such periods of time as the Trustees may deem fit;

(iv) to invest any or all of the funds of the Trust Estate in such manner as the Trustees, acting in their absolute discretion, deem fit;

(v) to deal with the Trust Estate generally for the benefit of the Beneficiaries;

(vi) to compromise, adjust, arbitrate, sue, institute, defend, abandon, settle or otherwise deal with proceedings of any kind on behalf of or against the Trust or the Trust Estate as the Trustees shall in their sole and absolute discretion deem fit;

(vii) to determine in a fair and reasonable manner whether any part of the Trust Estate, or any addition or increment thereto be income or principal, or whether any cost, charge, expense, tax, or assessment shall be charged against income or principal, or partially against income and partially against principal;

(viii)   to engage and compensate agents, accountants, brokers, attorneys-in-fact, attorneys-at-law, tax specialists, realtors, custodians, investment counsel, and other assistants and advisors, and to do so without liability for any neglect, omission, misconduct, or default of any such agent or professional representative, provided he or she was selected and retained with reasonable care;

(ix)   to vote any stock, shares, bonds, securities or any other voting rights held by the Trust or attributable to the Trust Estate; and to delegate such voting power in such manner as the Trustees may deem fit having regard to any legal requirements;

(x)   to consent to the reorganization, consolidation, merger, liquidation, readjustment of, or other change in any corporation, company, or association and to execute such documents and do all such acts and things as may reasonably be required to effect same;

(xi)   to engage in business with the Trust Estate property as sole proprietor, or as a general or limited partner, with all the powers customarily exercised by an individual so engaged in business, and to hold an undivided interest in any property as tenant in common or as tenant in partnership, to the extent permitted by law; and to enter into such agreements and contracts as the Trustee may deem necessary to regulate such businesses;

(xii)   to purchase securities, real estate, or other property from any party connected to the Grantors (or either of them), be it by contract or blood, provided such purchase is on an arm's length basis at market value and same is in the best interest of the Grantors and the Beneficiaries hereunder;

(xiii)   to make loans or advancements to any party connected to the Grantors (or either of them), be it by contract or blood, provided such loans and advancements are on an arm's length basis at market value and same are in the best interest of the Grantors and the Beneficiaries hereunder;

(xiv)   to act through an agent or attorney-in-fact, by and under a power of attorney duly executed by the Trustees to the extent permitted by law, in carrying out any of the authorized powers and duties; and

(xv)   to undertake such further acts as are incidental to any of the foregoing or are reasonably required to carry out the tenor, purpose and intent of the Trust.

7.2   The powers granted to the Trustees and Successor Trustee under Clause 7.1 may be exercised in whole or in part, from time to time, and shall be deemed to be supplementary to and not exclusive of the general powers of trustees pursuant to law, and shall include all powers necessary to carry them into effect.

7.3   Notwithstanding anything contained herein to the contrary, no powers enumerated or accorded to trustees generally pursuant to law shall be construed to enable the Grantors, or the Trustees or either of them, or any other person, to sell, purchase, exchange, or otherwise deal with or dispose of all or any part of the corpus or income of the trusts for less than an adequate consideration in money or money's worth, or to enable the Grantors to borrow all or any part of the corpus or income of the trusts, directly or indirectly, without adequate interest or security.

8.   SUCCESSOR TRUSTEE

8.1   On the death of or during any period of disability of either of the Grantors, the other Grantor shall serve as sole Trustee. In the event of the death or during any period of incapacity of both Grantors or the Surviving Grantor, _____ of _____ shall be appointed as Successor Trustee. In the event the aforementioned person is unable or unwilling to act as Successor Trustee, _____ of _____ shall serve as Successor Trustee.

8.2   If none of the persons named in Clause 8.1 are able and willing to act as successor trustee, then any nominated Successor Trustee may appoint (with preference going to the primary Successor Trustee's choice) a replacement successor trustee to serve as Successor Trustee hereunder provided that such appointment is made in writing, signed by the Successor Trustee making the appointment, notarized and forwarded to each of the named Beneficiaries. In the event that no Successor Trustee is willing and able to make such an appointment or in the event that the Successor Trustees fail to secure the appointment of a new Successor Trustee and notify the Beneficiaries of such appointment within 7 days of the declining Successor Trustee's refusal to act, then the next Successor Trustee shall be chosen by a majority in interest of the then living Beneficiaries, with a parent or guardian voting for each minor Beneficiary.

8.3   On acting, a Successor Trustee may, by notice in writing to the next Successor Trustee and to all Beneficiaries, resign from office at any time provided at least 14 days notice in writing of such resignation is provided. The resigning Successor Trustee shall prior to his or her resignation taking effect deliver an accounting of the assets, income and expenses of the Trust (and all sub-trusts, if any) to the next Successor Trustee. This accounting shall be made up to the date of resignation of the Successor Trustee. In the event of there being no readily identifiable Successor Trustee, the resigning Successor Trustee shall procure the appointment of a new Successor Trustee which may for the avoidance of doubt include a bank or trust company and shall notify the Beneficiaries in writing in the manner described in Clause 8.2 above. In the event that the Successor Trustee fails to secure the appointment of a new Successor Trustee and notify the Beneficiaries of same before the date of his or her resignation taking effect, then the next Successor Trustee shall be chosen by a majority in interest of the then living Beneficiaries, with a parent or guardian voting for each minor Beneficiary.

8.4   The appointment of the Successor Trustee under this Clause shall automatically terminate at the end of any period in which both Grantors were incapacitated but such termination shall not impact the automatic re-appointment of such Successor Trustee on the death of the Grantors or during any period of future incapacity of both Grantors or the Surviving Grantor, as contemplated by Clause 8.1.

8.5   A Successor Trustee shall (when validly acting in his/her capacity as successor trustee) be able to exercise all the powers of the Trustees hereunder including, for the avoidance of doubt, but not limited to, the powers of the Trustees referred to in Clause 3 to Clause 7 hereof as if he or she were a Trustee.

8.6   Trustees, Successor Trustee and their successors shall serve without bond. The Successor Trustees shall not be liable for any mistake or error of judgment in the administration of the Trust, except for willful misconduct, so long as they continue to exercise their duties and powers in a fiduciary capacity primarily in the interests of the Beneficiaries.

9.   REVOCATION AND AMENDMENT

9.1   Subject to Clause 4.4, the Grantors, or the survivor of them, shall acting jointly (or alone in the case of the Surviving Grantor) have the right and may by instrument in writing signed by each of the Grantors, or the survivor of them as the case may be, and delivered to the Trustees, modify or alter this Agreement, in whole or in part, without the consent of the Trustees, any beneficiary or any other party.

9.2   Subject to Clause 4.4, either of the Grantors, or the survivor of them, shall have the right and may by instrument in writing signed by either of them, or the survivor of them as the case may be, and delivered to the Trustees and the other Grantor, revoke this Agreement in whole without the consent of the other Grantor, the Trustees or any beneficiary.

9.3   Save as may otherwise be provided herein, the Trust shall not be amended, modified, revoked or terminated in any other way.

9.4   If the Trust is revoked, the Trustees shall promptly distribute the Trust Estate to the Grantors in such manner as would, as near as possible, restore the ownership of the Trust Estate to the manner in which it was held immediately prior to the transfer of the Trust Estate to the Trust.

10.   ADMINISTRATIVE PROVISIONS

10.1   The Trustees may at their absolute discretion, but shall not be obliged to, render an accounting at any time.

10.2   The Trustees waive the payment of any compensation for their services, but this waiver shall not apply to any Successor Trustee who qualifies and acts under this Agreement and who shall be entitled to reasonable compensation for his or her service.

10.3   This Trust has been accepted by the Trustees and will be administered in the State of _____ and its validity, construction, and all rights hereunder shall be governed by the laws of that State and that State shall have exclusive jurisdiction to determine any disputes which may arise hereunder.

IN WITNESS WHEREOF, the Grantors and Trustees have executed this Agreement on the date above written.

_____   _____
Signature of Grantor   Signature of Co-Grantor

_____   _____
Signature of Trustee   Signature of Co-Trustee

_____   _____
Name of First Witness   Signature of First Witness

_____   _____
Name of Second Witness   Signature of Second Witness

SCHEDULE ONE

Husband's Trust Property

SCHEDULE TWO

Wife's Trust Property

_____

_____

_____

_____

_____

_____

_____

_____

_____

_____

_____

_____

_____

_____

_____

_____

_____

_____

_____

_____

_____

_____

_____

_____

_____

_____

_____

_____

_____

_____

SCHEDULE THREE
Jointly Held Property

NOTARY AFFIDAVIT

STATE OF _____   **COUNTY OF** _____

On _____ before me, _____, a notary public, personally appeared _____ and _____, who proved to me on the basis of satisfactory evidence to be the persons whose names are subscribed to the within instrument and acknowledged to me that they executed the same in their authorized capacities, and that by their signatures on the instrument the persons executed the instrument. I certify under PENALTY OF PERJURY that the foregoing is true and correct.

Witness my hand and official seal.

Signature: _____

Print Name: _____

My commission expires on: _____

(Seal)

APPENDIX 4

MISCELLANEOUS CLAUSES FOR USE IN A REVOCABLE LIVING TRUST AGREEMENT

Custodianship Under UTMA

This clause should be placed in the property management section if required.

1.1   All property left under the terms of this revocable living trust to _____
shall be given to _____ of _____, in the capacity
of custodian of _____ under the [Insert State] Uniform Transfers
to Minors Act, to hold until _____ reaches __ years of age. If the
aforementioned person is unwilling or unable to serve as custodian for any reason, then
_____ of _____ shall be hereby appointed as custodian
instead.

Child's Sub-Trust

This clause should be placed in the property management section if required.

1.1.1   In the event that _____ has not reached the age of _____
years on the date of [Grantor Name]'s death, then any property left to him/
her under this revocable living trust shall be retained in a sub-trust and held,
managed and distributed for his/her benefit. The sub-trust shall be known as
the _____ sub-trust. The currentlt acting trustee (Whether the
original trustee or the successor trustee as the case may be) of the living trust
shall be trustee of this sub-trust. The sub-trust shall be managed by the trustee
in accordance with the provisions below.

If you wish to make a Sub-Trust for more than one person, just copy and paste
the above clause 1.1.1 in here, renumber it and then complete it in the same way
as clause 1.1.1.

1.1.2   So much of the income from an individual sub-trust and, if the net income be
at any time insufficient, so much of the principal of this sub-trust as may be
deemed necessary in the sole discretion of the trustee (taking into account all
other sources of income, support and circumstances of the sub-trust beneficiary
of which the trustee has knowledge) may be either paid to or expended on
behalf of the sub-trust beneficiary (whichever in the trustee's sole discretion is
deemed most appropriate) in order to ensure the support, maintenance, health,
and education (including collegiate, vocational, professional, etc.) of the sub-
trust beneficiary.

1.1.3   A sub-trust shall terminate on the earliest to occur of the following:

    (i)   when the sub-trust beneficiary reaches the age set out in the clause establishing that sub-trust beneficiary's sub-trust above, in which case the principal, together with any accumulations of income of the sub-trust, shall be paid over and distributed to the said sub-trust beneficiary; or

    (ii)   the sub-trust principal is exhausted through distributions validly made under the sub-trust provisions herein; or

    (iii)   on the death of the sub-trust beneficiary, in which case the property being held for that trust beneficiary shall be paid over and distributed (i) under the terms of the sub-trust beneficiary's Will, or in default of such, (ii) to the sub-trust beneficiary's issue (if any), per stirpes, or in default of such, (iii) to the sub-trust beneficiary's brothers and sisters and descendants of deceased brothers and sisters, per stirpes, or in default of such, (iv) to the gifting Grantor's heirs, determined as if he had died at the time of the sub-trust beneficiary's death pursuant to the General Statutes of _____.

1.2   No interest hereunder shall be transferable or assignable by any Beneficiary, or be subject during his or her life to the claims of his or her creditors.

1.3   Notwithstanding anything herein to the contrary, the trusts created under this Clause shall terminate not later than twenty-one (21) years after the death of the last Beneficiary named herein.

Appointment of Alternate Beneficiary of a Specific Gift

Below are sample clauses used to nominate alternate beneficiaries for specific gifts under a revocable living trust.

Single Trust

_____ of _____ shall be given _____. If the aforementioned person does not survive the Grantor or refuses this gift the said property shall be given to _____ of _____.

Shared or Couple's Trust

_____ of _____ shall be given _____. If the aforementioned person does not survive _____ or refuses this gift the said property shall be given to _____ of _____.

Gift of Residue to More than One Person – Single Trust

The clause below is a sample clause that can be used to distribute the residuary trust estate amongst more than one person. The successor trustee will be responsible for dividing the residuary trust estate in the percentages specified. In sub-clause (i) below, one alternate beneficiary is appointed.

In sub-clause (ii) below, a number of alternates are appointed and each will receive a specified percent of the primary beneficiary's estate if the primary beneficiary fails to survive the grantor.

You can decide how many alternates you wish to nominate (if any) for each primary beneficiary and use the appropriate clause.

4.1.1   Any of the Trust Estate not otherwise disposed of hereunder (the "Residue Trust Estate") shall be divided by the Successor Trustee(s) as follows:

(i)   _____% thereof shall be given to _____ of _____. In the event that the aforementioned person shall fail to survive the Grantor or refuses to accept this gift, his/her share of the Residue Trust Estate shall be given to _____ of _____ for his/her own use and benefit absolutely.

(ii)   _____% thereof shall be given to _____ of _____. In the event that the aforementioned person shall fail to survive the Grantor or refuses to accept this gift, his/her share of the Residue Trust Estate shall be divided by the Successor Trustee(s) as follows:

  i   _____% thereof shall be given to _____ of _____.

  ii   _____% thereof shall be given to _____ of _____.

Gift of Residue to One Person and Multiple Alternates – Single Trust

4.1.1   Any of the Trust Estate not otherwise disposed of hereunder (the "Residue Trust Estate") shall be given to _____ of _____ for _____'s own use and benefit absolutely. If the said _____ predeceases the Grantor or refuses to accept this gift then in that event _____'s share of the Residue Trust Estate shall be divided by the Successor Trustee(s) as follows:

(i)   ___% thereof shall be given to _____ of _____.

(ii)   ___% thereof shall be given to _____ of _____.

Gift of Residue to More than One Person – Shared or Couple's Trust

4.1.1   Any of _____'s Trust Estate not otherwise disposed of hereunder ("_____'s Residue Trust Estate") shall be divided by the Surviving Trustee or, if deceased, the Successor Trustee(s) as follows:

    (i)   ____% thereof shall be given to _____ of _____. In the event that the aforementioned person shall fail to survive this Grantor or refuses to accept this gift, his/her share of _____'s Residue Trust Estate shall be given to _____ of _____ for his/her own use and benefit absolutely.

    (ii)   ____% thereof shall be given to _____ of _____. In the event that the aforementioned person shall fail to survive this Grantor or refuses to accept this gift, his/her share of _____'s Residue Trust Estate shall be divided by the Surviving Trustee or, if deceased, the Successor Trustee(s) as follows:

        i   ____% thereof shall be given to _____ of _____.

        ii   ____% thereof shall be given to _____ of _____.

Gift of Residue to One Person and Multiple Alternates – Shared or Couple's Trust

4.1.1   Any of _____'s Trust Estate not otherwise disposed of hereunder ("_____'s Residue Trust Estate") shall be given to _____ of _____ for _____'s own use and benefit absolutely. If the said _____ predeceases the aforementioned Grantor or refuses to accept this gift then in that event his or her share of _____'s Residue Trust Estate shall be divided by the Surviving Trustee or, if deceased, the Successor Trustee(s) as follows:

    (i)   ___% thereof shall be given to _____ of _____.

(ii)   ___% thereof shall be given to _____ of _____.

APPENDIX 5

DEED OF ASSIGNMENT

DEED OF ASSIGNMENT FOR USE WITH AN INDIVIDUAL REVOCABLE LIVING TRUST

DATED THIS ____ DAY OF _____, 20___.

_____

(Assignor/Grantor)

and

_____

(Assignee/Trustee)

DEED OF ASSIGNMENT

www.enodare.com

THIS **DEED** is made on this _____ day of _____, 20___.

BETWEEN:

(1) _____ of _____ in his/her
capacity as grantor of the Trust (the "**Grantor**"); and

(2) _____ of _____ in his/her
capacity as trustee of the Trust (the "**Trustee**").

WHEREAS:

A. Pursuant to a Revocable Living Trust Agreement dated the _____ day of _____,
20___, made between the Grantor and the Trustee, the Grantor created a trust known as
_____ (the "Trust").

B. The Grantor is the legal and beneficial owner of the property described in Clause 1
below (the "Property").

C. The Grantor has agreed to assign all of the Grantor's rights, interests and entitlements in
the Property to the Trust and the Trustee has agreed to accept such assignment subject
to the terms and conditions of this Deed.

NOW THIS DEED WITNESSETH AS FOLLOWS:

1. **ASSIGNMENT OF PROPERTY**

1.1 For good and valuable consideration (the receipt of which is hereby acknowledged),
the Grantor hereby absolutely and unconditionally assigns all the Grantor's rights,
entitlements, interests in and to the following property:-

_____
_____
_____
_____
_____

to the Trustee, as trustee of the Trust.

2. **BINDING ON SUCCESSORS**

2.1   This Deed shall be binding upon and enure to the benefit of the respective parties hereto and their respective personal representatives and successors.

3.   **NOTICE**

3.1   Any notice or other communication given or made under this Deed shall be in writing and shall be delivered to the relevant party or sent by first class mail to the address of that party specified in this Deed or to such other address as may be notified hereunder by that party from time to time for this purpose.

3.2   Unless the contrary shall be proved, each such notice or communication shall be deemed to have been given, made and delivered, if by letter, 48 hours after posting or if by delivery, when left at the relevant address.

4.   **COUNTERPARTS**

4.1   This Deed may be executed in any number of counterparts and by the different parties hereto on separate counterparts each of which when executed and delivered shall constitute an original and all such counterparts together constituting but one and the same instrument.

5.   **SEVERABILITY**

5.1   Each of the provisions of this Deed is separate and severable and enforceable accordingly and if at any time any provision is adjudged by any court of competent jurisdiction to be void or unenforceable the validity, legality and enforceability of the remaining provisions hereof and of that provision in any other jurisdiction shall not in any way be affected or impaired thereby.

6.   **WHOLE AGREEMENT**

6.1   This Deed contains the whole agreement between the parties hereto relating to the matters provided for in this Deed and supersedes all previous deeds or agreements (if any) between such parties in respect of such matters and each of the parties to this Deed acknowledges that in agreeing to enter into this Deed it has not relied on any representations or warranties except for those contained in this Deed.

AS WITNESS the parties hereto have executed this document as a deed on the date appearing at the head hereof.

EXECUTED AND DELIVERED AS A DEED

By _____ (print name)

As Grantor and Trustee

_____

(Signature)

In the presence of:

_____

(Name of witness)

_____

(Signature)

DEED OF ASSIGNMENT FOR USE WITH A COUPLE'S REVOCABLE LIVING TRUST

DATED THIS ____ DAY OF _____, 20___.

_____ **AND** _____

(Assignors/Grantors)

and

_____ **AND** _____

(Assignees/Trustees)

DEED OF ASSIGNMENT

www.enodare.com

THIS **DEED** is made on this _____ day of _____, 20___.

BETWEEN:

(1) _____ of _____ and
_____ of _____ in their capacity
as grantors of the Trust (the "**Grantors**"); and

(2) _____ of _____ and
_____ of _____ in their capacity
as trustees of the Trust (the "**Trustees**").

WHEREAS:

A. Pursuant to a Revocable Living Trust Agreement dated the _____day of
_____, 20___, made between the Grantors and the Trustees, the Grantors
created a trust known as _____ (the "Trust").

B. The Grantors (or either of them) are the legal and beneficial owners of the property
described in Clause 1 below (the "Property").

C. The Grantors have agreed to assign all of their respective rights, interests and
entitlements in the Property to the Trust and the Trustees have agreed to accept such
assignment subject to the terms and conditions of this Deed.

NOW THIS DEED WITNESSETH AS FOLLOWS:

1. **ASSIGNMENT OF PROPERTY**

1.1 For good and valuable consideration (the receipt of which is hereby acknowledged),
the Grantors hereby absolutely and unconditionally assign all of their respective rights,
entitlements, interests in and to the following property:-

_____

_____

_____

_____

_____

_____

to the Trustees, as trustees of the Trust.

2.   **BINDING ON SUCCESSORS**

2.1   This Deed shall be binding upon and enure to the benefit of the respective parties hereto and their respective personal representatives and successors.

3.   **NOTICE**

3.1   Any notice or other communication given or made under this Deed shall be in writing and shall be delivered to the relevant party or sent by first class mail to the address of that party specified in this Deed or to such other address as may be notified hereunder by that party from time to time for this purpose.

3.2   Unless the contrary shall be proved, each such notice or communication shall be deemed to have been given, made and delivered, if by letter, 48 hours after posting or if by delivery, when left at the relevant address.

4.   **COUNTERPARTS**

4.1   This Deed may be executed in any number of counterparts and by the different parties hereto on separate counterparts each of which when executed and delivered shall constitute an original and all such counterparts together constituting but one and the same instrument.

5.   **SEVERABILITY**

5.1   Each of the provisions of this Deed is separate and severable and enforceable accordingly and if at any time any provision is adjudged by any court of competent jurisdiction to be void or unenforceable the validity, legality and enforceability of the remaining provisions hereof and of that provision in any other jurisdiction shall not in any way be affected or impaired thereby.

6.   **WHOLE AGREEMENT**

6.1   This Deed contains the whole agreement between the parties hereto relating to the matters provided for in this Deed and supersedes all previous deeds or agreements (if any) between such parties in respect of such matters and each of the parties to this Deed acknowledges that in agreeing to enter into this Deed it has not relied on any representations or warranties except for those contained in this Deed.

AS **WITNESS** the parties hereto have executed this document as a deed on the date appearing at the head hereof.

EXECUTED AND DELIVERED AS A DEED

By _____ (print name)

As Grantor and Trustee

_____
(Signature)

In the presence of:

_____
(Name of witness)

_____
(Signature)

EXECUTED AND DELIVERED AS A DEED

By _____ (print name)

As Grantor and Trustee

_____
(Signature)

In the presence of:

_____
(Name of witness)

_____
(Signature)

APPENDIX 6

NOTICE OF REVOCATION OF A LIVING TRUST

DATED THIS ____ DAY OF _____, 20___.

NOTICE OF REVOCATION

of

_____

(Grantor)

NOTICE OF REVOCATION

I, _____ of _____, as grantor under a Revocable Living Trust Agreement dated the _____ day of _____, 20____ (the "Agreement") wherein you are designated as a trustee, or have been appointed successor trustee thereunder, do hereby revoke the powers and trusts created and conferred by me under the terms of the Agreement.

I hereby direct you, as trustee, to turn over and deliver to me all property held by you subject to the terms and provisions of the Agreement and to which I am entitled following this revocation, together with all accumulations of interest and income and any rights to which I am or ought to be beneficially entitled.

This REVOCATION is made this the _____ day of _____, 20__.

_____

GRANTOR

NOTARY AFFIDAVIT

STATE OF _____   **COUNTY OF** _____

On _____ before me, _____, a notary public, personally appeared _____, who proved to me on the basis of satisfactory evidence to be the person whose name is subscribed to the within instrument and acknowledged to me that he/she executed the same in his/her authorized capacity, and that by his/her signature on the instrument the person executed the instrument. I certify under PENALTY OF PERJURY that the foregoing is true and correct. Witness my hand and official seal.

Signature: _____

Print Name: _____

My commission expires on: _____

(Seal)

Other Great Books from Enodare's Estate Planning Series

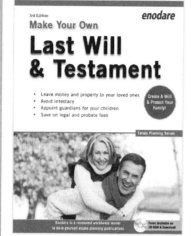

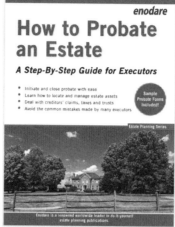

Make Your Own Last Will & Testament

By making a will, you can provide for the distribution of your assets to your love ones, appoint guardians to care for your children, provide for the management of gifts to young adults and children, specify how your debts are to be paid following your death, make funeral arrangements and much more.

This book will guide you through the entire process of making a will. It contains all the forms that you will need to make a valid legal will, simply and easily.

How to Probate an Estate - A Step-By-Step Guide for Executors

This book is essential reading for anyone contemplating acting as an executor of someone's estate!

Learn about the various stages of probate and what an executor needs to do at each stage to successfully navigate his way through to closing the estate and distributing the deceased's assets.

You will learn how an executor initiates probate, locates and manages assets, deals with debt and taxes, distributes assets, and much more. This is a fantastic step-by-step guide through the entire process!

Make Your Own Living Will

Do you want a say in what life sustaining medical treatments you receive during periods in which you are incapacitated and either in a permanent state of unconsciousness or suffering from a terminal illness? Well if so, you must have a living will!

This book will introduce you to living wills, the types of medical procedures that they cover, the matters that you need to consider when making them and, of course, provide you with all the relevant forms you need to make your own living will!

www.enodare.com

Other Great Books from Enodare's Estate Planning Series

 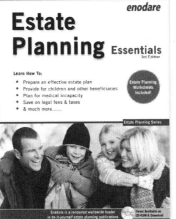 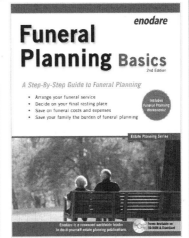

Make Your Own Medical & Financial Powers of Attorney	**Estate Planning Essentials**	**Funeral Planning Basics - A Step-By-Step Guide to Funeral Planning**

The importance of having powers of attorney is often underappreciated. They allow people you trust to manage your property and financial affairs during periods in which you are incapacitated; as well as make medical decisions on your behalf based on the instructions in your power of attorney document. This ensures that your affairs don't go unmanaged and you don't receive any unwanted medical treatments.

This book provides all the necessary documents and step-by-step instructions to make a power of attorney to cover virtually any situation!

This book is a must read for anyone who doesn't already have a comprehensive estate plan.

It will show you the importance of having wills, trusts, powers of attorney and living wills in your estate plan. You will learn about the probate process, why people are so keen to avoid it and lots of simple methods you can actually use to do so. You will learn about reducing estate taxes and how best to provide for young beneficiaries and children.

This book is a great way to get you started on the way to making your own estate plan.

Through proper funeral planning, you can ensure that your loved ones are not confronted with the unnecessary burden of having to plan a funeral at a time which is already very traumatic for them.

This book will introduce you to issues such as organ donations, purchasing caskets, cremation, burial, purchasing grave plots, organization of funeral services, legal and financial issues, costs of pre-arranging a funeral, how to save money on funerals, how to finance funerals and much more.

Will Writer - Estate Planning Software

Everything You Need to Create Your Estate Plan

Product Description

Enodare's Estate Planning Software helps you create wills, living trusts, living wills, powers of attorney and more from the comfort of your own home and without the staggering legal fees!

Through the use of a simple question and answer process, we'll guide you step-by-step through the process of preparing your chosen document. It only takes a few minutes of your time and comprehensive help and information is available at every stage of the process.

Product Features:

Last Wills

Make gifts to your family, friends and charities, make funeral arrangements, appoint executors, appoint guardians to care for your minor children, make property management arrangements for young beneficiaries, release people from debts, and much more.

Living Trusts

Make gifts to your family and friends, make property management arrangements for young beneficiaries, transfer assets tax efficiently with AB Trusts, and much more.

Living Wills

Instruct doctors as to your choices regarding the receipt or non-receipt of medical treatments designed to prolong your life.

www.enodare.com

Healthcare Power of Attorney

Appoint someone you trust to make medical decisions for you if you become mentally incapacitated.

Ensure Your Family's Protected

 ### Power of Attorney for Finance and Property

Appoint someone you trust to manage your financial affairs if you become mentally incapacitated, or if you are unable to do so for any reason.

 ### And More.........

Enodare's Will Writer software also includes documents such as self proving Affidavits, Deeds of Assignment, Certifications of Trust, Estate Planning Worksheet, Revocation forms and more.

The documents are valid in all states except Louisiana.

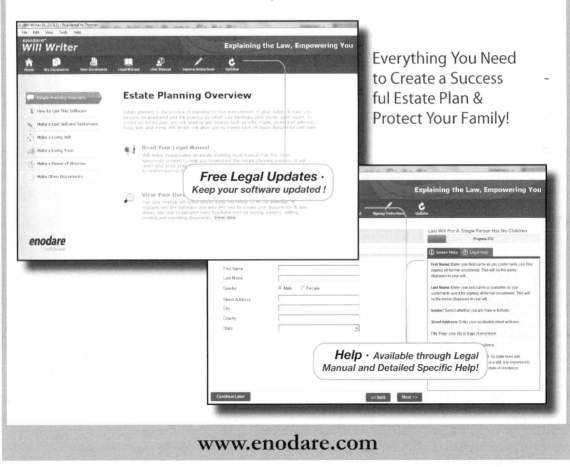

Everything You Need to Create a Success - ful Estate Plan & Protect Your Family!

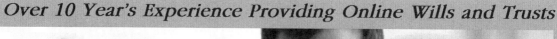

Entrepreneur's Guide to Starting a Business

Entrepreneur's Guide to Starting a Business takes the fear of the unknown out of starting your new business and provides a treasure chest of information that will help you be successful from the very start.

First-time entrepreneurs face a daunting challenge in identifying all of the issues that must be addressed and mastered when starting a new business. If any item slips through the cracks, or is handled improperly, it could bring a new company crashing to the ground. Entrepreneur's Guide to Starting a Business helps you meet that challenge by walking you through all of the important aspects of successfully launching your own business.

When you finish reading this book, not alone will you know the step-by-step process needed to turn your business idea and vision into a successful reality, but you'll also have a wealth of practical knowledge about corporate structures, business & marketing plans, e-commerce, hiring staff & external advisors, finding commercial property, sales & marketing, legal & financial matters, tax and much more.

- Comprehensive overview of all major aspects of starting a new business

- Covers every stage of the process, from writing your business plan to marketing and selling your new product

- Plain English descriptions of complex subject matters

- Real-world case study showing you how things play out in an actual new business environment

Personal Budget Kit

Budgeting Made Easy

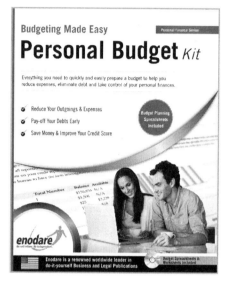

In this kit, we'll guide you step-by-step through the process of creating and living with a personal budget. We'll show you how analyze how you receive and spend your money and to set goals, both short and long-term.

You'll learn how to gain control of your personal cash flow. You'll discover when you need to make adjustments to your budget and how to do it wisely. Most of all, this kit will show you that budgeting isn't simply about adding limitations to your living but rather the foundation for living better by maximizing the resources you have.

This Personal Budget Kit provides you with step-by-step instructions, detailed information and all the budget worksheets and spreadsheets necessary to identify and understand your spending habits, reduce your expenses, set goals, prepare personal budgets, monitor your progress and take control over your finances.

- Reduce your spending painlessly and effortlessly

- Pay off your debts early

- Improve your credit rating

- Save & invest money

- Set & achieve financial goals

- Eliminate financial worries

Budget Planning Spreadsheets Included